AF324251

ACHIEVING VICTORY—WORLD WAR II

ALSO BY MONRO MacCLOSKEY

Your Future in the Air Force
How to Qualify for the Service Academies
Reserve Officers Training Corps
You and the Draft
NATO, Guardian of Peace and Security
The 885th Bomb Squadron (Heavy Special) in World War II—Two Volumes
Secret Air Missions
Pacts for Peace
The Infamous Wall of Berlin
The U.S. Air Force, Its Roles and Missions
The American Intelligence Community
From Gasbags to Spaceships
Hallowed Ground, Our National Cemeteries
Our National Attic
Alert the Fifth Force
Reilly's Battery
Planning for Victory, World War II

Achieving Victory— World War II

A Behind-the-Scenes Account

MONRO MacCLOSKEY
BRIGADIER GENERAL, USAF (RET.)

RICHARDS ROSEN PRESS, INC., NEW YORK 10010

Standard Book Number: 8239-0192-0
Library of Congress Catalog Card Number: 72-116617

Published in 1970 by Richards Rosen Press, Inc.
29 East 21st Street, New York City, N.Y. 10010

First Edition

Manufactured in the United States of America

Dedication

To the working-level members of the Anglo-American
military planning staffs in Washington, London, and
Algiers during World War II, whose plans for military
strategy at times seemed superficial and futile but
contributed enormously to the grand strategy
of winning the war.

General of the Army George Catlett Marshall, Chief of Staff, U.S. Army, 1 September 1939–18 November 1945.

About the Author

Brigadier General Monro MacCloskey, USAF (ret.) a command and jet pilot, began his career in 1920 as a West Point Cadet, graduating in 1924. Shortly after the outbreak of World War II, he was ordered to England as a member of the staff charged with organizing the 12th Air Force and planning the invasion of North Africa. He participated in the first assault landing in North Africa and later became Deputy to the Assistant Chief of Staff for Operations in the 12th Air Force, with headquarters in Algiers.

In the course of the war, General MacCloskey held a wide variety of posts, including those as Chief of Organization, Training, and Equipping Section, Operations Division, Northwest African Air Force; a member of the Joint Planning Staff of the Mediterranean Air Command; and Assistant Director of Plans for the Mediterranean Allied Air Force. He organized, equipped, trained, and commanded the 885th Bomb Squadron (H) Special of the 15th Air Force, which engaged in the night dropping of resistance personnel and supplies into Southern France, Northern Italy, and the Balkans; and the 15th (later redesignated the 2641st) Special Group, which performed similar functions throughout Europe. In addition, General MacCloskey flew fifty combat missions.

After the war, General MacCloskey attended the National War College and upon graduation was appointed Chief of the Air Intelligence Policy Division at AF Headquarters. He served as Air Attaché to France, Belgium, and Luxembourg, and at the time of his retirement was Commander of the 28th Air Division, Air Defense Command.

His World War II decorations include the Silver Star; Legion of Merit with Cluster; Distinguished Flying Cross; Air Medal with seven Clusters; EAME (Europe-Africa-Middle East) Medal with nine Stars and one Arrowhead; Army Commendation Medal with Cluster; two French Croix de Guerre with Palm and two with Gold Star; two French Legion of Honor, one Degree of Officer and one Degree of

Commander; Order of the Partisan Star; and Decoration of the Sultan of Morocco.

General MacCloskey is now Executive Director of the Air Force Historical Foundation, with headquarters at Bolling Air Force Base, D.C.

Contents

Foreword   11

   I. *Worldwide Deployment of U.S. Forces*   15
   II. *Operation "ANVIL Modified"*   28
 III. *Preparations for OVERLORD*   44
 IV. *Decline of the CBI Theater*   58
   V. *Secondary War in the Pacific*   72
 VI. *The London Conference*   85
VII. *Postwar Political Problems*   105
VIII. *OCTAGON, the Second Quebec Conference*   123
 IX. *Strategic Survey of the War against Germany and Japan*   139
   X. *Epilogue*   157

Appendices
   I. *Glossary of Abbreviations*   170
   II. *Glossary of Code Names*   172
 III. *Minutes of Meetings of COSSAC Mission and JPS Algiers*   174

Table: U.S. Overseas Deployment, Dec. 31, 1943   24–25

List of Illustrations
   General George Catlett Marshall   Frontispiece
   General Dwight D. Eisenhower   45
   Allied Invasion Chiefs   86
   Visitors at the Normandy Beachhead   89
   President Roosevelt at the Pearl Harbor Conference   99
   Guard of Honor at the OCTAGON Conference   125
   President Roosevelt and Prime Minister Churchill at Casablanca   133

Foreword

This is a behind-the-scenes account of wartime national planning in the field of American military strategy. National planning in that area covers the spectrum from simple statements of risks and options to the complete analysis of an immense undertaking. Strategic decisions are seldom made and military operations are rarely conducted in the exact terms worked out by the international planning staffs. The conquest of Sicily was such an example. Nevertheless, broad outline planning, which on occasions seemed an exercise in futility to the staffs, is the principal instrument that enables political leadership to reach an agreement between the compulsions of politics and the realities of war, to exercise control over military operations, and to allocate the means to support the operations.

The attitude and policy of the United States toward alliances have undergone a revolutionary reversal within a generation. The United States has passed from its traditional suspicion and fear of "entangling alliances" to a policy that stakes its security and interests on the co-operation of other powers. In World War I the United States cautiously defined its relationship with the powers allied against Germany as that of an Associated Power. Although the last to join the Grand Alliance in World War II, the United States virtually integrated its resources with those of the British Commonwealth and coordinated its strategy and war aims with the British and the U.S.S.R. in the most powerful wartime partnership ever forged.

This book is a narrative of national strategic planning and its trials and tribulations in the midwar period of World War II. It is not to be considered as a comprehensive treatise on national planning. Rather it is a story of the discussions, debates, arguments, frustrations, and triumphs of the wartime strategic planners as they faced the problems of coalition warfare. The complicated issues that confronted General George C. Marshall, Chief of Staff, U.S. Army, and his principal staff advisers in reconciling U.S. Army views on strategy with those of the Navy and Army Air Forces, and integrating American and British views and adjusting them to the military policies of the Soviet Union are presented. No attempt has been made, however, to cover in full the positions of the other partners in the Alliance. It was during that troubled midwar period that the great international conferences were held and the Allied Powers formulated their grand strategy for achieving military victory.

Planning for Victory, World War II, also by this writer dealt with strategic planning in the midwar era through December 1943. It recounted the plans and dispositions of U.S. armed forces in the defensive phase of coalition warfare, and presented a behind-the-scenes account of planning by General Marshall and his staff in the debates and discussions on European and Pacific strategy that followed the Allied landings in North Africa through the Cairo-Tehran meetings in November-December 1943.

This volume is also a contribution to the study of wartime national planning and military strategy. It follows the plans, issues, and decisions from the SEXTANT Conference to the end of the summer of 1944, when the problems of winning the war began to encounter the challenges of victory and peace. Again the presentation utilizes a narrative approach, setting forth the principal steps in the development of the American strategic position. It endeavors to give an account of the debates and discussions that took place as decisions on plans and concepts were achieved within the American military staff, the Joint Chiefs of Staff, the Combined Chiefs of Staff, and—at the plenary sessions—the heads of government.

The climax of America's most intensive experience with coalition strategy occurred in the period of World War II described in this book. They therefore should have a special interest for all who are concerned with the implications of the revolution in U.S. foreign policy that has taken place in the twentieth century.

Authors and historians who write on the subject of strategic planning are usually venturing into an area that is generally familiar only to a few career professional officers, and to them through their training and personal experience. The author of this book falls into that relatively small group of officers. He participated as a member of a working committee in the 1941 American-British staff talks and later in the ARCADIA Conference. He was a member of the U.S. staff in London that planned the invasion of French North Africa. Subsequently he was the U.S. Army Air Forces member of the Joint Planning Staff, Mediterranean Theater of Operations, in Algiers that examined all conceivable military operations that could be mounted in that theater, and prepared in broad outline those plans that were to be implemented. He was also one of the JPS delegates from Algiers who participated as a working member at the Cairo-Tehran Conference.

This book has been written after extensive research of the great volume of documentary material in the National Archives and Records Service, and in the documents and records of the Departments of the Army, Navy, and Air Force, and the library of the Air Force Historical Foundation.

The author gratefully acknowledges the assistance rendered by many individuals in the Department of Defense and National Archives in providing excellent reference materials.

MONRO MacCLOSKEY
Brigadier General, USAF (ret.)

Chapter **I**

Worldwide Deployment of U.S. Forces

Two years after Pearl Harbor, Allied strategy for the war against Germany had finally been established at the SEXTANT Conference. OVERLORD was to be the supreme effort of the Western Allies in Europe to defeat Germany by striking directly at the heart of Hitler's Reich. The principles that shaped OVERLORD were developed early in World War II, but their application was interrupted by improvisation and diffuse experimentation. Although British and American planners worked together, they also worked separately, particularly in the early war years. Their efforts paralleled each other at times, whereas at other times they were at cross-purposes. Furthermore, divergent opinions struggled for acceptance within both the British and American military establishments. After SEXTANT the U.S. planners aimed to amass the men and resources necessary for the invasion of the Continent.

By the end of 1943 the changing requirements and circumstances of coalition warfare had greatly affected the plans and programs for expanding the U.S. armed forces—both in total strength and in overseas deployment. Although the U.S. Army grew from 5,397,674 to 7,482,434 during 1943, it was appreciated by the Army planners that there was a bottom to the manpower barrel. As long as military and civilian production were maintained at a high level, the bottom of the barrel would not be reached, and the Army felt no need to urge a reduction in the American standard of living. The Federal Government continued to grant industrial and agricultural deferments to draftees, and the Army solved its manpower problems by such internal economies as reducing the number and strength of overhead establishments and garrisons and the requirements for combat forces.

In November 1943 President Roosevelt approved a total strength for the Army of 7,700,000. That quota was not reached until March 1944 because of manpower shortages and the inability of the Office of Selective Service to meet the requirement. By the end of 1943 the Army not only had large groups of soldiers studying in colleges under the Army Specialized Training Program who could not be immediately utilized, but it was more than 200,000 men short of the authorized strength.

Early in 1943 the Army troop basis was set at 8,208,000. The November ceiling was achieved by a decision that 90 divisions were necessary to win the war. In January 1943 there were 74 divisions: 52 infantry, 2 cavalry, 14 armored, 2 airborne, and 4 motorized. During 1943 the trend was toward increasing infantry and airborne divisions, not only to meet tactical and strategic requirements, but also to save shipping space by using forces not completely motorized or so heavily armed. As a result, by January 1944 there were 90 divisions: 67 infantry, 2 cavalry, 16 armored, and 5 airborne.

During 1943 the number of trained divisions in the United States greatly increased, largely because of a lack of strategic decisions on the conduct of the multifront war, the overtaxed port facilities, and the imbalances of shipping. Training camps were overcrowded, and lack of suitable facilities made activation of additional divisions difficult. Seventeen divisions were shipped overseas during 1942 as compared to only 13 in 1943. The 60 divisions left in the United States were neither fully manned nor equipped, since they provided replacements for divisions overseas, and the equipping of French divisions had a higher priority than the new divisions. In late 1943 manpower requirements for the B-29 operations, the rotation program, and the Army Specialized Training Program (which was being conducted on a reduced basis) eliminated any possibility of activating another 15 divisions in 1944.

The successful operations of the Russians on the Eastern Front and the increasing effectiveness of the Combined Bomber Offensive changed the composition of the Army in favor of air and service troops because fewer U.S. ground troops than originally planned would be required to defeat the Axis. The 90-division limit on ground forces permitted a greater proportion of the 1943 manpower strength to flow into the air and service forces. During that buildup period the intensification of the air war against both Germany and Japan and the development of the long lines of worldwide communications continued to increase the air and service totals. By the end of 1943 the Air Corps strength was 1,810,900, an increase of

42 percent; those in the service forces totaled 2,735,076, an increase of 47 percent; and the strength of the ground arms was 2,451,007, an increase of 26 percent. So, for the first time in the war, the strength of the service forces was greater than that of the ground arms.

The limitation of the number of ground combat troops brought up the replacement problem. Until most of the ground combat units were deployed to combat areas, they would be called upon to supply personnel and equipment replacements for divisions already engaged in combat. With OVERLORD on the horizon, the problem would have to be solved by the planners if an adequate, trained strategic reserve were to be immediately available in case of possible reverses.

Despite persistent shipping imbalances and the lack of strategic direction, the total overseas deployment of the Army increased from 17 divisions and 72 air groups (total strength 1,064,643) to 30 divisions and 136 air groups (total strength 2,618,075) during 1943. In that same year the strength of the Army deployed overseas against Germany and Japan increased 275 percent to 2,329,407:

British Isles	768,274
Mediterranean	597,658
Africa, Middle East (including	
Persian Gulf Command)	50,553
Pacific	696,847
China-Burma-India	94,560
Alaska	121,535

Those figures tell the story of the course of the U.S. war effort in 1943: increasing deployment to the Mediterranean and Pacific, mounting costs of the China commitment, and neglect of the buildup for OVERLORD.

Deployment to the Mediterranean and Middle East

The deployment of U.S. Army forces in the Mediterranean, which began with TORCH in November 1942, increased steadily until November 1943. Initially the Americans had been reluctant to expand operations in the Mediterranean area. Nevertheless, the trained, experienced forces already in the area and the political and military advantages of defeating German air and ground forces in Sicily and Italy created pressures that resulted in further operations in the Mediterranean. The momentum of the Allied effort in the North African campaigns led to the conquest of Sicily and the invasion of Italy.

Those campaigns required additional U.S. forces. In December 1942, a total of 227,092 U.S. troops were engaged in the TORCH operation. One year later, when the combat area was in Italy, the number of U.S. troops in the Mediterranean had increased to 597,658.

The increase in personnel, however, was not in the ground combat troops but in the number of air and service troops. The Army Air Forces expanded from 25 to 41 groups with a strength of 142,790, which was about one fourth the total in the area, and the aircraft strength was more than tripled. The air forces in the Mediterranean provided air support for ground operations and for supplying the Italian partisan forces, and were part of the Combined Bomber Offensive, since they could launch strikes against targets that were beyond the range of bomber units operating from bases in the United Kingdom.

As a result of changes in war planning, the Mediterranean theater began to lose some U.S. divisions to the U.K. in late 1943. In December 1942 there were 6 U.S. divisions in the Mediterranean. Three additional divisions arrived, increasing the total to 9 in September 1943. But by the end of 1943, 4 divisions were transferred to the U.K. and only one new division arrived from the United States—leaving 6 divisions in the theater, the same strength as that with which the year began.

The Middle East was an area of British responsibility, and the United States endeavored to remain free of the internal problems of the area and to keep its military forces at a minimum. Their strength increased from 30,850 to 50,553 during 1943. However, the Allied advance northward in Italy enabled the United States to reduce its commitments to the British in the Middle East. In the meantime it had become important for the United States to aid the Soviet Union; therefore, the increase in U.S. military strength in the Middle East in 1943 was used to assist the development of the U.S. command to supply Russia over the southern route. In December 1943 the Persian Gulf Service Command was separated from the U.S. Army forces in the Middle East and was redesignated the Persian Gulf Command, a separate entity.

Deployment to the U.K.

The U.S. military planners established a program early in 1943 for the deployment of 1,026,000 men to the U.K. by 1944. The military requirements of the Pacific and the Mediterranean, the close shipping schedules, and the fact that there were no ground operations in the theater all tended to preclude the planned expansion.

The expanded Combined Bomber Offensive and the arrival of 4 divisions from the Mediterranean in late 1943 helped toward the projected goal, but the strength of 768,274 at the end of 1943 was far short of the programmed strength of 1,026,000. Only one U.S. division was stationed in the U.K. in December 1942, and it remained the only major U.S. ground force in the U.K. until July 1943. Ten more divisions arrived during the remainder of the year.

Army Air Forces in the U.K. expanded from 15 air groups in December 1942 to 52 groups during 1943. Almost 40 percent (294,385) of the total military personnel stationed in the U.K. were in the AAF. At the same time the aircraft strength practically quintupled; but it was decided at the SEXTANT Conference to mount OVERLORD and to give top priority to the buildup of U.S. ground and air forces in the U.K.

Deployment to China-Burma-India

The China-Burma-India Theater was a rather complicated tangle of military, political, and jurisdictional problems. The Allies had recaptured very little territory from the Japanese on the Asiatic mainland, yet the continuous expansion of the American commitment to the CBI during 1943 caused an increase of over 500 percent in the number of troops stationed there. The expansion to 94,560 in December 1943 from 17,087 in December 1942 indicated the increasing costs involved in sustaining the Chinese in the war against Japan. The United States regarded the CBI as primarily an air and service theater and had agreed to open an overland line of communications to China. In the meantime the U.S. was attempting to establish an airlift operation. The complexities of the line of communications and the mounting requirements of the airlift required constantly increasing manpower. As the prospective B-29 operations neared, further manpower demands appeared inevitable. No U.S. combat divisions were stationed in CBI in 1943, only AAF and service troops.

At the end of December 1942, 4 AAF groups and one separate squadron were in the CBI. One year later there were 7 air groups and 6 separate squadrons, a strength of over 40,000 personnel in the theater, and the number of aircraft had more than tripled. Logistics, however, was the big problem for the Army in China and until it was resolved, the size of the air forces under Major General Claire L. Chennault (U.S. Commander of the China Air Task Force) would be limited. The arrival of B-29 groups would further complicate the supply problem.

Overseas Deployment in the Western Hemisphere

When the manpower situation grew acute early in 1943, General George C. Marshall, Chief of Staff, U.S. Army, ordered a survey of all defense garrisons and a reduction wherever possible. As a result, the Caribbean Defense Command, which had grown to 119,286 troops by December 1942, was cut to 91,466 by the end of the following year. The number of air groups assigned to the Caribbean was reduced from 9 to 2. Actually it was only a reduction on paper because the group designations were dropped and large separate squadrons were organized. The threat of submarine attacks and the possibility of sea raids required the retaining of air forces for the protection of the southern sea frontier.

Alaska was similarly affected. The military strength of the Alaskan Command during 1943 had grown from 96,061 in January to 148,167 in August when operations against Kiska were undertaken. After the Japanese left the Aleutian Islands in July, there was a steady drop in military strength. By the end of 1943 there were only 121,535 personnel assigned. Two AAF groups were stationed in Alaska during 1943, but the number of squadrons in those groups was reduced from 10 to 6 and the number of assigned aircraft was decreased. The declining importance of overseas garrisons in the Western Hemisphere reflected the views of the War Department that the "shooting war" had passed them by.

Deployment in the Pacific

In the Pacific the American forces moved from the defensive phase of warfare to the offensive phase. The change was accomplished by a continuous deployment of Army forces from the United States. Like the TORCH operation, the Guadalcanal Campaign had been offensive as well as defensive in nature, and as the momentum gathered force, each moved forward to new objectives. During 1943 British pressures at the international conferences for extending operations in the Mediterranean were countered by American pressures for operations in the Pacific, where the strength of the U.S. forces was increased steadily.

During 1943 the allied forces moved forward step by step in the South and Southwest Pacific. They advanced to Bougainville in the Solomon Islands and to the Huon Peninsula in New Guinea. As the year ended they were invading New Britain in the Southwest Pacific, and American forces were conducting an amphibious sweep in the Central Pacific with the invasion of the Gilbert Islands. In 1943 the Army's forces in the Pacific increased from 350,720 to 696,847, a considerable increase over that originally scheduled by the planners.

At the end of 1942, 9 Army divisions were stationed in the Pacific: 4 were in the Central Pacific; 3 in the South Pacific, and 2 in the Southwest Pacific. During 1943, 4 divisions arrived in the Pacific: 3 for the Central Pacific, one of which came from Alaska; one from Hawaii for the South Pacific, and 2 for the Southwest Pacific, one also coming from Hawaii. The 4 divisions from the United States were in place by midsummer of 1943. At the same time the number of air groups in the Pacific increased from 17 to 32, and the number of aircraft more than doubled. The number of light and medium bombers, essential for the advance in New Guinea and through the Solomon Islands, nearly quadrupled. The strength of the Army Air Forces personnel increased to 162,376, roughly 23 percent of the total Army strength in the Pacific.

The buildup and deployment of Army forces in the Pacific created a tremendous problem in logistics. The long distances, the shortage of base and communications facilities, port delays, and the imbalances in shipping affected the nature and extent of U.S. deployment in that ocean theater. For each combat division sent to the area, twice as many service troops were required for supply and transportation. With the launching of the Central Pacific drive late in 1943, requirements for the Pacific area would continue to increase in preparation for the more powerful amphibious assaults and long-range B-29 bombing attacks of 1944.

In Summary

To recapitulate, during 1943 almost 1,500,000 American Army troops were deployed overseas. Those included 13 Army divisions and 8,516 Army Air Forces aircraft. More than two thirds of those totals, or approximately 1,000,000 troops, 9 divisions, and 6,000 aircraft were deployed against Germany. When those totals are combined with the totals shipped overseas during 1941–42, it is obvious that the main war effort was to be directed against Germany. As indicated on the following table, the cumulative totals at the end of 1943 showed 1,416,485 men, including 17 divisions and 8,237 aircraft, deployed against Germany as opposed to 912,942 troops, including 13 divisions and 4,254 aircraft, against Japan. That was in sharp contrast to the Army forces deployed overseas at the end of 1942, when the manpower strength and number of divisions and aircraft opposing Japan exceeded those lined up against Germany.

The Army deployment statistics for 1943 were in agreement with the Allied strategic concept that the main effort of the Allied forces should first be committed to the defeat of Germany, then brought to bear against Japan. About 10 percent of the Army personnel and 65 percent of the Army Air Forces planes deployed against Germany and Japan were now opposing Germany. Whereas 17 divisions were deployed against Germany as compared with 13 divisions against Japan, the European buildup of divisions was just on the point of a rapid expansion, and the trend of faster expansion in the Pacific in 1942 was now reversed. Actually it was not until October 1943 that the number of divisions in Europe exceeded those in the Pacific–Far East. That was because of failure of the Allies to agree upon a specific plan for the cross-Channel assault until the SEXTANT Conference. As a consequence, a more rapid deployment of forces against Japan had occurred than had been anticipated by the planners early in 1943.

In addition to the figures quoted above, the accompanying table of U.S. Overseas Development shows the effort expended by the U.S. Navy and Marine Corps in fighting the multifront war. The foregoing brief approximation of the overseas war effort at the end of 1943 may dispel somewhat the illusion that the Pacific–Far East was being neglected during the second year of the war. General Douglas Mac-Arthur, commander of U.S. Armed Forces in the Far East, and Admiral Chester W. Nimitz, commander of U.S. Naval Forces in the Pacific, except those assigned to task forces by the Joint Chiefs of Staff (JCS), were not being required to fight on a shoestring, in contrast to the European commanders. After two years of war, U.S. forces and resources were fairly well balanced between the European and Japanese fronts.

The table shows greater U.S. manpower strength against Japan than against Europe, but the number of divisions was slightly greater against Europe. Also, more aircraft were operating against Germany, most of them four-engine bombers. The European theaters also had more transport aircraft assigned—849 as compared with 545. The latter figure does not include 165 aircraft of the Air Transport Command, which were flying the Hump airlift. If added to the 545, they would bring the total to 710, which narrows the spread considerably.

Most of the newest combat ships of the U.S. Navy were operating in the Pacific. Although Navy and Marine Corps personnel made up only 22 percent of the U.S. effort against Germany, they composed more than half of all U.S. forces in the Pacific. In the distribution of aircraft, 46 percent of those operating in the Pacific were assigned to the Navy or Marine Corps, whereas only 6 percent of those in the Atlantic-Mediterranean belonged to the Navy.

As regards shipping under Army control, 549 ships, totaling 4,924,558 measurement tons and a troop capacity of 353,948, were on the Atlantic-Mediterranean run. In the Pacific–Far East there were 437 ships, totaling 3,837,287 measurement tons and a troop capacity of 160,590. War Shipping Administration (WSA) cargo ships allocated to the Army and Navy as of Jan. 1, 1944, totaled 5,300,000 deadweight tons in the Atlantic and 4,290,000 deadweight tons in the Pacific. Thus the Army and WSA allocations gave the European theaters about 55 percent of the shipping under their control. Those figures do not include statistics of cargo ships controlled outright by the Navy. In view of the preponderance of the naval effort in the Pacific, their inclusion might very well change the percentage ratios. Unfortunately, the statistics on the distribution of cargo shipping under Navy control at the end of 1943 are not available. Nor is there a complete breakdown on overall distribution of landing craft and combat loaders in all categories.

However, there was a preponderance of attack transports, attack cargo ships, and landing ships (tanks) in the Pacific at the end of 1943, and the Europrean theaters had more landing craft (infantry). The shortages in landing craft were perplexing. When the 1942 production program was completed early in 1943, no new program was established by the staff planners. Destroyer escorts and other vessels urgently needed to combat the submarine menace in the Atlantic were given top priority. Despite the discussions at QUADRANT on landing craft for OVERLORD and for Pacific operations, a lull occurred in construction during the summer of 1943, particularly in the larger types of landing craft. Increases were approved in landing craft construction by the JCS during September and October, but since the increases would be small until early in 1944, OVERLORD would get little benefit from that action. In December, after SEXTANT, another increase in production was approved, but it was earmarked primarily for the Pacific. The tardiness in deciding to expedite the program, the delays inherent in the shipyards converting to landing craft production, changes in design, winter weather, and the overcrowded conditions prevailing in the shipyards delayed construction at the end of 1943—just when time was at a premium. The prospects for achieving the goals set at SEXTANT were not very bright.

Why the landing craft shortage was permitted to develop and grow

U.S. Overseas Deployment: 31 December 1943

		Against Germany				Against Japan			
	Total	European theater[a]	Mediter-ranean theater	Middle East theater[b]	Atlantic Ocean[c]	Total	Pacific[d]	CBI	Alaska
Personnel	1,810,367	805,792	615,958	50,553	338,064	1,878,152	1,629,023	94,660	154,469
Army[e]	979,310	473,889	454,868	50,553	0	688,711	534,471	52,624	101,616
Air Forces[f]	437,175	294,385	142,790	(g)	0	224,231	162,376	41,936	19,919
Navy[h]	391,400	36,400	18,300	(g)	336,700	804,800	772,800	100	31,900
Marine[h]	2,482	1,118	0	0	1,364	160,410	159,376	0	1,034
Divisions	17	11	6	0	0	16+	16+	0	0
Army	17	11	6	0	0	13	13	0	0
Marine	0	0	0	0	0	3+	3+	0	0
Aircraft	8,807	(i)	(i)	(i)	(i)	7,857	(i)	(i)	(i)
Army	8,237	4,618	3,619	(g)	0	4,254	3,073	933	248
Heavy bombers	2,263	1,686	577	(g)	0	716	532	167	17
Medium bombers	1,084	444	640	(g)	0	544	428	84	32
Light bombers	167	53	114	(g)	0	179	179	0	0
Fighters	3,456	1,866	1,590	(g)	0	1,897	1,327	422	148
Reconnaissance	268	193	75	(g)	0	152	93	58	1
Transports	849	253	596	(g)	0	545	427	79	39
Miscellaneous	150	123	27	(g)	0	221	87	123	11
Navy	570	(i)	(i)	(i)	(i)	3,603	(i)	(i)	(i)
Bombers	204	(i)	(i)	(i)	(i)	1,098	(i)	(i)	(i)
Fighters	0	(i)	(i)	(i)	(i)	564	(i)	(i)	(i)
Carrier aircraft	366	(i)	(i)	(i)	(i)	1,941	(i)	(i)	(i)

Combat ships	515		713	
Battleships	6	2 new, 4 old[j]	13	6 new, 7 old
Aircraft carriers	10	1 large, 9 escort	28	7 large, 7 light, 14 escort
Cruisers	10	2 heavy, 3 light, 5 old light	32	12 large, 13 light, 2 antiaircraft, 5 old light
Destroyers	120	80 new, 40 old	188	175 new, 13 old
Submarines	40	6 new, 34 old	123	105 new, 18 old
Destroyer escorts	112	112 new	57	57 new
LST's	92	92 new	125	125 new
LCI's	110	110 new	99	99 new
Attack transports (APA)	10	10 new	34	34 new
Attack cargo (AKA)	5	5 new	14	14 new

[a] Includes Iceland.

[b] Includes Persian Gulf Command.

[c] South Atlantic Naval Forces.

[d] Includes SWPA, SOPAC, and CPA totals for the Army and POA totals for the Navy and Marine Corps.

[e] All Army (including ground and service forces) personnel figures are based on STM–30, Strength of the Army, 1 January 1948.

[f] Air Forces personnel and aircraft figures are based on AAF Statistical Digest, 1945, and USAF Statistical Digest, 1947.

[g] Air Forces and Navy personnel in the Middle East Theater are included in the Mediterranean Theater totals.

[h] All Navy and Marine figures are based upon planners' estimates in JCS 521/3, 4 February 1944, title: Strategic Deployment of U.S. Forces to 31 December 1944. Navy figures include both shore-based and ship-based personnel. Marine figures for 31 December 1943—furnished by the Office of Navy Comptroller—show 5,827 marines in Atlantic area and 156,507 in the Pacific. It has been impossible to reconcile Navy figures currently available with the planners' estimates.

is not clear from the record. The War Production Board discerned the need for increased production in August 1943. The delay in establishing a new and enlarged program until the fall of 1943 was possibly the fault of the principal strategic planners for not anticipating the requirements of 1944 soon enough to enable the shipyards to prepare for the new demands. Other considerations, however, were involved in the problem. The uncertainty about OVERLORD and Mediterranean operations had not been finally resolved at QUADRANT. The submarine menace that had led to the establishment of the high priority destroyer and escort vessel program in the spring of 1943 had diminished, but was still a concern to the planners. Furthermore, the Navy continued to protect diligently the production and allocation of landing craft destined for the Pacific. That action stemmed from the unsettling effects that the 1942 landing craft program had had upon the Navy's overall construction program. It was not until the close of 1943, when the Allied heads of government had reached a resolute decision on the war against Germany, that the strategic and logistical planners could proceed with full confidence that the cross-Channel assault would take place.

*   *   *

Some of the implications of engaging in a multifront war become more obvious when the statistics on the distribution of U.S. manpower and resources are considered. It is manifest that designating the conflict in one area as a primary war and the other a secondary war was not adequate. The events of 1942 and 1943 provided abundant evidence that a policy of opportunism in the multifront war tended to invalidate paper priorities and led to diversions usually unfavorable to projected long-range deployment projects. Limited and secondary offensives, covered by such catch phrases as "maintaining the strategic initiative" and "applying unremitting pressure," continued to absorb more men and resources than originally planned, frequently at the expense of long-range buildups. The staff planners had learned through experience that it was impossible to keep a secondary war secondary as long as no definite and accepted long-range plan existed for the primary war. The tendency to expand subordinate operations in the absence of overall decisions assigning top priority to the main effort was hard to resist.

Further, after two years of participation in the war, the United States had acquired a number of "fixed charges" that were accorded preferential treatment in the allocation of U.S. resources—the basic understandings of which consisted of maintaining America's Allies.

Added to the diversions of the secondary fronts were such charges as provision for the security of the Western Hemisphere and the British Isles, fulfillment of the Soviet protocols, and aid to China, France, and Italy. It was not until OVERLORD was given top priority by the three heads of government at SEXTANT that it could compete with other basic undertakings for U.S. resources. The multifront war could finally be resolved into the primary conflict of defeating Germany first, as had been planned by the War Department staff in the early stages of the coalition war.

Chapter II

Operation "ANVIL Modified"

Following the conclusion of the last Cairo meeting in December 1943, British and Americans returned to Washington, London, and Algiers to carry out the decisions reached at SEXTANT. One of the first directives issued by Allied Force Headquarters follows:

ALLIED FORCE HEADQUARTERS

29 December 1943.

SUBJECT: Operation ANVIL.
TO   :   Commander-in-Chief, Mediterranean.
Air Commander-in-Chief, Mediterranean.

1. In accordance with the instructions of the Combined Chiefs of Staff an operation in conjunction with OVERLORD will be launched against the south coast of FRANCE, with the object of establishing a bridgehead in the area and subsequently to exploit towards LYON and VICHY, with a target date during May 1944.

2. The code name allotted to this operation is ANVIL.

3. It is not at present possible to say what assault shipping and craft will be allotted for the operation but it may be taken that a lift for at least two divisions will be available.

4. The ground forces engaged in the operation will be American and French. The exact proportion of each cannot yet be definitely decided but it is likely to be in the region of four American and six French divisions. Of this total not more than two of the divisions will be armored and these will be French.

5. Naval forces for the operation will be provided by the Commander-in-Chief, Mediterranean.

6. Air Forces for this operation will be provided by the Air

Commander-in-Chief Mediterranean from resources available in the M.A.A.F.

7. In calculating forces available it should be assumed that two RCT of airborne personnel will be available, with lift for one RCT at a time.

8. Details of the personnel and MT shipping likely to be available for the operation will be notified to you later.

9. A copy of the instructions issued to the Army Commander entrusted with this operation will be forwarded immediately this officer is nominated. Commander-in-Chief Mediterranean is requested to nominate immediately a Naval Commander for the operation. The Air Commander-in-Chief Mediterranean is requested to issue instructions to the Air Commanders and to nominate immediately the Air Commander responsible for providing air protection and close air support to the assault.

10. Planning will be carried out at the ECOLE NORMALE, BOUZAREAH. Further details as to date for assembly of planning staffs will be notified to you in due course.

11. A copy of an appreciation with annexes and draft outline plan as prepared by the Joint Planning Staff at AFHQ is forwarded for any help which this may be to the Task Force Commanders nominated.

12. Once Task Force Commanders have been nominated instructions as to date of submission of their outline plan will be notified.

(Signed: J. F. M. Whitely, Maj. Gen.)
W. B. SMITH
Major General, U.S. Army,
Chief of Staff.

On Jan. 1, 1944, orders were issued by AFHQ appointing Lieutenant General Mark W. Clark, U.S. Army, commander of the ground forces taking part in ANVIL. Instructions were issued by Headquarters Mediterranean Allied Air Forces on Dec. 28, 1943, to commanders of air organizations directing their participation in Operation ANVIL.

One of the documents prepared during December 1943 by the JPS Algiers was the Appreciation and Outline Plan for ANVIL (P/122 dated 21 December 1943). The document was restudied in January with the result that a new planning paper (P/124, "ANVIL Modified") was prepared on Jan. 23. It was approved by the Chief of Staff, AFHQ, three days later and delivered to the Army and

Air commanders for operational planning. Section I of the modified ANVIL reads as follows:

ALLIED FORCE HEADQUARTERS
G-3 SECTION

23 January 1944

OPERATION ANVIL (Modified)
Section I—Appreciation

1. *OBJECT.*

To prepare an outline plan for an operation to be launched in conjunction with OVERLORD against Southern FRANCE, target date at the beginning of May, 1944, with a lift for an assault of one division and a planned build up of up to nine divisions, and with provision for subsequent exploitation northwards.

2. *ASSUMPTIONS.*

    a. On the mainland, the Allies are confronting the PISA-RIMINI line. To the extent possible, without detracting from ANVIL, pressure is being maintained in ITALY.

    b. Other forces in the Mediterranean are not engaged in offensive operations elsewhere.

    c. The force to include a US Corps of two infantry divisions. The remaining forces to be French.

3. *SHAEF CONSIDERATIONS.*

SHAEF stipulates the following conditions in preparation of ANVIL:

    a. No amphibious assault may be launched prior to D day OVERLORD.

    b. That forces should exploit northwards towards LYON and VICHY, a distance of about 225 miles.

4. *CONCEPTION OF THE OPERATION.*

All information as to terrain, ports, beaches etc. in the South of FRANCE will be found in P/122 (Tab A). [Omitted.] It will be possible to consider utilizing areas of beach in ANVIL (Modified) which were too small to be considered in the original conception of the plan.

The following extract from MAF 492 gives the situation regarding the effect of ANVIL (Modified) as envisaged last October, and in the main still stands true for today. Such modifications as have resulted from subsequent events and further examination are discussed in this paper.

"13. *Effect of a Landing.*

In view of its small size, and slow build up, the Mediterranean diversion cannot expect to establish itself ashore until it becomes apparent that the opposition will not be sufficient to overrun it prior to the arrival of reinforcing troops. We cannot therefore expect to land the expedition until the Germans withdraw part of their forces from the South of FRANCE. Thus the expedition cannot reasonably expect to fulfill, by landing, the primary object of this diversion—to prevent the Germans from withdrawing forces from Southern FRANCE—during the critical days of the OVERLORD operation. I consider that more German divisions are likely to be contained in Southern FRANCE by the mounting of a threat on as large a scale as possible than by the actual launching of an operation which, after the first 48 hours, will have displayed its weakness. The resources in this theater should, with the assistance of carefully conceived plans, enable a considerable threat to be mounted and maintained. SHAEF consider that it will probably become apparent to the Germans somewhere between $D - 40$ and $D - 30$ that an assault is to be launched from UK against Western EUROPE. SHAEF wishes that the threat from the Mediterranean should first become apparent to the Germans at $D - 6$ weeks, should gradually increase in scope, and should be maintained until about $D + 21$.

"14. *Actual Assault.*

Although I consider that a threat will assist OVERLORD more than would an assault on or about D day, it will be essential to put the force ashore as soon as the situation permits; this may occur as a result of weakening value of our threat with consequent German withdrawals Northwards, or in consequence of successful Allied action against the German forces in the North.

It will therefore be necessary to prepare the expedition fully for an assault, and to hold it at immediate readiness."

5. *SELECTION OF THE ASSAULT AREA*

In view of the above and from information available in P/122, it is clear that a series of alternative areas must be considered. The final choice of area must be dependent on the situation at the time, the progress of OVERLORD, and the wishes of SHAEF. The areas which it is considered offer the best prospects to meet the different conditions which may be pertaining at the time, and brief descriptions of the conditions under which they may prove to be most suitable, are given below.

a. Area of beach 2.3 miles south of MARSEILLE.
b. RADE de BORMES–CAP CAMARAT.
c. FREJUS–ST. RAPHAEL.
d. CANNES.
e. NICE.

Beach ⅔ miles South of MARSEILLE
The advantage of this area is that it lies immediately south of the port which it is desired to develop as our main base. The coast defenses in the area are the heaviest of any in Southern FRANCE, with the result that it would only be possible to assault there when the defenses had been drastically reduced and conditions similar to RANKIN existed.

NOTE: The RADE D'HYERES, which was selected for the assault in the original ANVIL plan, is less strongly defended than the MARSEILLE area, but it is nevertheless too strongly defended for a small scale attack to succeed there until the fixed defenses are considerably reduced.

If therefore conditions do exist which permit an assault against either of these highly defended areas, then the MARSEILLE area offers the greater advantages.

RADE DE BORMES–CAP CAMARAT
The defenses in this area are on a considerably lighter scale than those near MARSEILLE. On the other hand the area lies (according to the exact area chosen) between 25–52 miles from TOULON and 70–97 miles from MARSEILLE; in addition there is no ready made airfield in the vicinity. There is no port within this area.

FREJUS–ST. RAPHAEL
This area is some 60 miles from TOULON and 105 from MARSEILLE. There is an airfield just by the coast. The defenses are lighter than those in the area already considered.

ST. RAPHAEL is a port of 300 tons per day capacity only suitable for small ships.

CANNES and NICE

These areas are respectively 130 and 165 miles from TOULON. Their defenses are about on the same scale as the FREJUS–ST. RAPHAEL area and both places have an airfield in the neighborhood.

The NICE area however possesses a natural defensive flank in the form of the ALPS on the east. A landing in this area would therefore possess the advantage that the portion of the bridgehead for which defenses would be required would be considerably less than in any other area under consideration. In addition the NICE area is farther away from the estimated station areas of any of the mobile reserves. As a result the arrival of these reserves to counter a landing would be a few hours later than for any other area.

CANNES has a capacity of 600 tons per day, and is suitable for coasters only. NICE is 2500 tons per day capacity and can take ships up to 22′ draft. The anchorage space off NICE is severely restricted and the rate of follow up over the beaches from MT ships might be limited by this factor.

6. *ENEMY ACTION.*

It is likely that process of reduction of German strength in Southern FRANCE will be:

   a. Withdrawal of his mobile divisions.
   b. Destruction of ports, airfields, communications.
   c. Withdrawal of coastal divisions and reduction of coast defenses.

7. *DISCUSSION AS TO ASSAULT AREA.*

With an assault of one division it is considered that a decision to land in Southern FRANCE would only be made if it was thought that a landing would do more to contain German divisions in the South of FRANCE than the continuance of a threat, or the situation in Southern FRANCE developed into RANKIN conditions. A critical situation in OVERLORD might justify the ANVIL assault even though the operation appeared to have small chance of success. The fact that the Allies succeeded in establishing themselves in Southern FRANCE might have important political effects and stimulate the resistance movements to large scale effort.

If RANKIN conditions existed in Southern FRANCE the assault would obviously be made in the MARSEILLE area.

If, on the other hand, RANKIN conditions did not exist and it was decided that a landing was required, the assault area could be selected from one of the following:

   a. RADE de BORMES–CAVALIERE
   b. FREJUS–ST. RAPHAEL
   c. CANNES–NICE

The descriptions of these areas as given in para 5 show that the RADE de BORMES–CAVALIERE has the single advantage over the other areas listed in that it is nearer to a major port. The advantage does not, it is considered, compensate for the disadvantages inherent in this area. The choice is therefore limited to *b* and *c*.

The particular characteristics of both these areas lead to the conclusion that, whereas it would be possible to effect a successful landing in NICE with the present estimated strength of German opposition, a landing in the ST. RAPHAEL area could only be made after the enemy mobile reserves have withdrawn.

The advantages of being able to land in the NICE area earlier than elsewhere is somewhat offset by the possibility that relatively small forces might contain such a landing and prevent prompt exploitation from the bridgehead.

On balance, however, in order to keep the operation as simple as possible and avoid the necessity for alternative plans, to make use of such port facilities as exist in either of these areas and to permit of a landing at the earliest possible moment, it is considered that NICE should be the area selected for the operation. A decision to land near MARSEILLE would of itself imply that opposition would be negligible. In such circumstances the assault force mounted to land at NICE would only require slight additional information and issue of maps to make it suitable for a landing in this alternative area.

Conclusions.

From the above we conclude that plans should be laid to meet two possible cases:

Case I.

That the progress of OVERLORD demands an actual landing at the earliest possible moment without waiting for a reduction of the German ability to oppose the assault. In these circumstances we should land in the NICE area.

NOTE: If at the time ANVIL is mounted, the Allies on the
Italian mainland are north of the PISA-RIMINI
line (see assumption (a) to this paper), it is considered that the NICE (or CANNES) area should
be selected for the assault.

Case II.

That conditions are such that the threat from the Mediterranean is sufficient assistance to OVERLORD in its early
stages in which case we should wait for the actual landing
until the MARSEILLE defenses are reduced sufficiently to
allow us to land there.

8. *AVAILABILITY OF FORCES.*
   a. *Ground*

   In order to provide the contemplated size of force, it will
   be necessary to withdraw all the French formations from
   the mainland of ITALY. If this is done, some seven
   French divisions, including two armored divisions, should
   be available in time.

   It is considered that the assault should be made by a
   battle trained US division ex ITALY. It is likely that
   this division would require to be withdrawn in time to
   receive the necessary training at the I.T.C. and refit.
   This move has already been ordered.
   b. *Naval and Air.* (For details see P/122). [Omitted.]

9. *BUILD UP.*
   a. *Own Forces.*

   With assault shipping and craft available for one division, and on the assumption that the SEXTANT allocation of MT/Store shipping is available, it is estimated that we should be able to obtain the following
   build up of forces.
   D Day—one div (at 25,000 men and 4,000 vehicles)
   D + 2 —2 divs plus 1 RCT (at 25,000 men and 4,000
   vehicles per div and 4,300 men and 420
   vehicles for the RCT)
   D + 4 —3 divs (at above scale)
   D + 6 —3 divs plus 1 RCT
   D + 16—4 divs (at 28,000 men and 4,800 vehicles)
   D + 28—5 divs (at 30,000 men and 5,400 vehicles)

Thereafter, owing to the non-availability of service units, the build up is likely to be very slow.

b. Enemy.

In P/122 it was estimated that the enemy would have up to seven infantry divisions defending the South coast of FRANCE with up to two mobile divisions in reserve. If these mobile divisions have not been withdrawn the enemy build up would be as shown in P/122, para 11. [Omitted.]

If our attack is withheld until the mobile reserve has been withdrawn the enemy build up would be as follows:

Period	*Arriving during period*	*Available end of period*
D		1 Inf Div
D–D + 4	Elements 1 Inf Div	1–2 Inf Divs
D + 5–D + 10	Elements 1 Inf Div	Equiv 3 Inf Divs

10. *MOUNTING AND STAGING.*
    a. *Assault:* This force should be staged in CORSICA and/or SARDINIA.
    b. Follow up: Follow up divisions, except one US, will be French. In order to reduce movement to the minimum, they should be mounted if possible from their station areas. These areas are likely to be: two inf divs from ITALY, one inf div from CORSICA, three inf and two armd divisions from North AFRICA.

11. *ACTION AFTER THE ASSAULT.*

The form of operations once the assault has got ashore is likely to fall into three phases:

Case A when landing is made in MARSEILLE area.
Phase I—Establishment of a bridgehead around assault area.
Phase II—Extension of secured bridgehead to include MARSEILLE.

Case B when landing is made in the NICE area.
Phase I—Establishment of a bridgehead around the assault area.
Phase II—Exploitation to secure the port of TOULON.

> Phase III—Operations to secure the port of MAR-
> SEILLE.

It is considered that any major exploitation northward is likely to have to wait until after the port of MARSEILLE has been opened to our shipping.

12. *ADMINISTRATION.*

P/122 and Annex X to that paper deal fully with the administrative aspects of this operation, other than the tonnages which will be somewhat different. At Appendix A to this appreciation is a tabulation of the tonnages which it is estimated must be put ashore in this modified operation. [Omitted.]

13. *PLANNING AND COMMAND.*

Since the Planning Staff for Operation ANVIL has already been set up and is already planning and since ANVIL Modified deals generally with the same area and largely with the same troops, it is recommended that ANVIL Modified be planned and commanded by Force 163.

14. *CONCLUSIONS.*

The majority of the conclusions given in P/122 apply to this appreciation. Owing however to the fact that ANVIL (Modified) only envisages an assault by one division the following conclusions differ from those listed in P/122.

    a. Smaller areas of beach will be suitable for the assault than could be considered in P/122.

    b. Unless RANKIN conditions exist no attempt can be made to land in the highly defended areas of MARSEILLE or the RADE D'HYERES.

    c. In order to be in a position to land as early as possible plans should be prepared to assault in the NICE area.

    d. An assault could be made in the NICE area at any time provided the enemy scale of build up did not exceed that laid down in P/122.

    e. A landing in the MARSEILLE area would facilitate the capture of the port of MARSEILLE and create an opportunity for a rapid build up for exploitation up the RHONE Valley. If, however, the scale of German resistance makes a landing in the above area unlikely to succeed the assault should be made in the NICE area.

    f. The decision to plan an assault in the NICE area would be suitable for an operation in conjunction with the Allied Forces in ITALY, should the latter be north of the PISA-RIMINI line at the time ANVIL (Modified) is launched.

g. Plans prepared for an assault in the NICE area could be simply adapted for a landing in the MARSEILLE area.

h. The assault should be made with a battle tested US division.

i. The Commander and Staff for this operation should be Force 163.

15. Section II, attached hereto, is an outline plan of one method by which the ANVIL Modified operation might be carried out.

OUTLINE PLAN FOR OPERATION ANVIL

1. Two plans are submitted:
PLAN A for an assault of two divisions.
PLAN B for an assault of three divisions.
2. The plans are divided into:
PART I   Preliminary Phase.
PART II   Preparatory Phase.
PART III   Assault and capture of a port.
PART IV   Operations after the capture of a port.

PART I—PRELIMINARY PHASE
(Common to Plans A and B)

1. This phase is already in being. All efforts are being directed to carrying out such air action (especially POINTBLANK), sea action, propaganda, political and economic pressure and sabotage as is calculated to soften the degree of German resistance.

PART II—PREPARATORY PHASE

1. *a. Air action prior to the assault.*
Air action to neutralize the enemy air forces by the bombing of airfields within effective range of the assault area will be initiated approximately D − 42, continued and intensified as necessary up to and throughout the operation.

A bombing program designed to assist the operation and impair the enemy's ability to counter the assault will also be undertaken. Care will be necessary not to jeopardize surprise. Photographic and reconnaissance requirements will be completed during this phase, and a counter-radar program initiated at the appropriate time.

As **D** day approaches, there must be a withdrawal of air forces from other commitments, except those of a purely defensive character, in order to insure that the maximum effort can be exerted in support of the ANVIL operation during the initial phase.

b. Naval and ground action during this period calls for no comment.

PART III—ASSAULT AND CAPTURE OF A PORT

TIMING.

1. The final decision as to the timing of the ANVIL assault must be the result of consultation with COSSAC.

It was agreed with COSSAC before SEXTANT that no expedition should sail for Southern FRANCE until it is known with certainty that OVERLORD is sailing from UK. On this assumption the ANVIL assault would not take place before OVERLORD D + 3 to D + 4.

DIVERSIONS.

2. All available assault shipping and craft will be required for the main assault; therefore none will be available for staging any major diversionary operations.

This will not preclude minor diversions which will be for consideration during detailed planning.

NEUTRALIZATION OF DEFENSES.

3. Owing to the fact that area selected for the assault (RADE D'HYERES) is flanked by a series of defended islands it will be necessary for the defenses on those islands to be neutralized before the assaulting forces can be landed on the beaches.

Subsidiary landings by Commandos and Rangers would be undertaken both on those islands and on the mainland in the CAP BENAT area (and possibly at CAP NEGRE for Plan B) prior to the assault with a view to neutralizing the defenses thereon.

AIR OUTLINE PLAN.

4. Air cover during the approach and the assault will be provided by land based fighters operating from CORSICA and pos-

sibly SARDINIA, possibly supplemented by aircraft operating from aircraft carriers. Bombing attacks against enemy airfields will be continued as necessary as a primary requirement. All other fighter-bomber and bomber effort available will be directed against targets selected with a view to assisting the assault and impeding the enemy's counter-measures. It will be difficult during this phase for fleeting or other targets to be attacked at short notice on call.

Reconnaissance and photographic reconnaissance requirements will be met. Anti-submarine, counter-radar, and other planned programs will be put into effect. Airborne operations, if required, can be undertaken up to the capacity of the Troop Carrier units in the Command.

At Appendix 1 to these plans is a brief appreciation as to a method of operating escort carriers in this operation. [Omitted.]

NAVAL OUTLINE PLAN.

5. Since no opposition is possible from an enemy battle fleet, the main feature of the naval plan is the convoy program necessary to meet the requirements of the assault and follow up. Outline convoy program for Plans A and B are attached at Appendix 2. [Omitted.] This Appendix also shows the escort requirements for the two plans, including the requirement for a force of four escort carriers.

Provision must also be made for fire support by naval gunfire. It is expected that one old French battleship; some twelve British, American and French cruisers, light cruisers and contre-torpilleurs, and the equivalent of a flotilla of destroyers, will be available for this purpose.

This force will also provide cover against any interference with the assault forces by enemy light naval forces.

ARMY OUTLINE PLAN.

6. *a. The Assault.*

   (1) *Pre H hour action.* (Common to Plans A & B)
     Commandos or Rangers will land from assault craft to neutralize the defenses in the areas:—
     CAP BENAT
     Ile de PORQUEROLLES
     Ile de PORT CROS
     Ile de LEVANT
     GIENS
     CAP NEGRE (in case of three div assault)

(2) *Plan A* (Two divisional assault)
   Landing.
   (i) Two simultaneous assaults will be made:—
      (a) One division on Western beaches of RADE D'HYERES.
      (b) One division on Northern beaches of RADE D'HYERES.
      The approximate assault areas are shown on the map at Appendix 3 [omitted] to the plan. Exact areas can only be decided as a result of detailed examination of the beaches.
   (ii) Each assaulting division will be on a two RCT front. An immediate follow up will consist of the third RCT of each assaulting division, plus one further RCT from the Corps.
   (iii) Each RCT landed in the assault and immediate follow up will have a proportion of tanks (10 approx).

Object.
To establish a bridgehead in two phases:—
Phase I—To be captured by D + 1.
General Line—See map at Appendix 3. [Omitted.]
Phase II—To be captured by D + 2.
General Line—See map at Appendix 3. [Omitted.]
(3) *Plan B* (Three divisional assault)
   Landing.
   (i) Three simultaneous assaults will be made:—
      (a) One division on Western beaches of RADE D'HYERES.
      (b) One division on Northern beaches of RADE D'HYERES.
      (c) One division in the **CAP BENAT** area.
      The approximate assault areas are shown on the map at Appendix 3 [omitted], attached to this plan. Exact areas can only be decided as a result of detailed examination of the beaches.
   (ii) Each assaulting division will be on a two RCT front. An immediate follow up will consist of the third RCT of each assaulting division.
   (iii) Each RCT landed in the assault and immediate follow up will have a proportion of tanks. (10)

Object.
To establish a bridgehead in two phases.
Phase I—To be captured by D + 1.
General Line—See map at Appendix 3. [Omitted.]
Phase II—To be captured by D + 2.
General Line—See map at Appendix 3. [Omitted.]

b. *Build up.*
   Ground.
   A very rapid initial build up is necessary to give greater insurance for a successful operation. This is achieved by using LST after they have landed their initial load, to ferry vehicles ashore from two successful flights of pre-loaded MT ships.
   It is estimated that build up may be in the order of:—

   With assault shipping and craft for two divisions:
     2 divisions ashore on D day.
     5 divisions ashore by D + 3 (@ 25,000 men and 4,000
                       vehicles per division)
     6 divisions ashore by D + 12.
   10 divisions ashore by D + 80 (@ 45,000 men and
                       8,000 vehicles per
                       division)

   With assault shipping and craft for three divisions:
   The force landed in D day to D + 3 period can be increased to about 5½ divisions, and the build up to 10 divisions can be completed by about D + 68.

   Air.
   The rate of build up will depend upon the rate of advance of land forces and the availability of airfields. It is the intention to attain as rapid a build up as possible of fighter and fighter-bomber units, followed by light and medium bomber units, if the tactical situation allows.

c. *Capture of TOULON.* (Common to Plans A & B)
   One French infantry division and one French armored division to be landed by morning D + 3. Provided the security of a satisfactory bridgehead these formations to form a striking force to exploit westwards and capture TOULON by D + 5.

d. *Use of Airborne Forces in the Assault.* (Common to Plans A & B)

(1) One RCT airborne force to land immediately prior to the assaulting forces in the area of CUERS (0311), with the object of delaying enemy reinforcements of the assault area and obtaining lodgement in the extended bridgehead.

(2) This RCT to be withdrawn immediately Phase II of the bridgehead has been established.

(3) One RCT Airborne forces to be held as reserve.

e. *SOE/OSS Operations.*

At Appendix 5 are outline plans which would be put into operation in conjunction with the main ANVIL plan. [Omitted.]

f. *Administration.*

At Appendix 4 is an outline administrative plan for the operation. [Omitted.]

PART IV—OPERATIONS SUBSEQUENT TO THE CAPTURE OF TOULON

1. The development of operations after the security of the TOULON bridgehead has been insured will necessarily be conditioned, as to timing, to a great extent by the enemy resistance and known enemy movement; our object, at this stage, will be to seize the port of MARSEILLE directly our military position vis-a-vis that of the enemy allows us to do so.

2. Once MARSEILLE has been secured the object will be to exploit northward with a view to gaining control of the LYON-VICHY area.

*   *   *

P/124 did not conclude the examination of the JPS on ANVIL Modified. A memorandum was received from the Deputy Chief of Staff, AFHQ, on Feb. 27 for a complete reexamination of the operation.

Chapter III

Preparations for OVERLORD

After a brief trip to the United States to confer with President Roosevelt and War Department officials, General Eisenhower arrived in London on Jan. 14 to take up his new duties as Supreme Commander, Allied Expeditionary Force. The expanded COSSAC staff became Supreme Headquarters, Allied Expeditionary Force (SHAEF). The main lines of strategy for the second front against Germany had been established at SEXTANT, and the invasion of France from the west was the primary undertaking for 1944. OVERLORD was to be the greatest amphibious operation in history and the mightiest Allied commitment of the war. The twenty weeks that remained before the troops were loaded in ships for the fateful thrust across the Channel were weeks of decision when the plans, studies, suggestions, and experience acquired during the past three years were translated into operational directives.

Despite an almost unbroken chain of Allied victories during 1943, Germany was anything but defeated. Civilian morale was still good, and the German military forces gave no indication of weakening. The Allied advance in Italy had been halted by a combination of winter weather, difficult terrain, and stiff resistance by German forces. By November 1943 Hitler realized that the invasion of Western Europe might begin at any time. Whenever a crisis arose theretofore for which fresh troops were required, Hitler had drawn them from Western Europe. The campaign in Italy, the threat to the Balkans, and the losses on the Eastern Front had necessitated pulling out the best German divisions. On Nov. 3, 1943, Hitler informed his commanders that he could no longer weaken his position in Western Europe in favor of other theaters of war. He further advised them that forces and defenses in the west would be strengthened to throw

U.S. ARMY PHOTOGRAPH

General Dwight D. Eisenhower, Supreme Allied Commander, Supreme Headquarters, Allied Expeditionary Force, and Commanding General, U.S. Forces, European Theater of Operations.

the expected invasion back into the sea, or, if worst came to worst, to contain it on the beachhead.

By the spring of 1944, when Field Marshal Erwin Rommel assumed command of the defenses of Western Europe, the German troops that had been withdrawn had been largely replaced. German agents in the British Embassy at Ankara had in the meantime learned the meaning of the code word OVERLORD, and the German High Command concluded that the major Allied assault would be in Western Europe and not in the Balkans. Although the Germans did not know the time and place of the invasion, they endeavored to complete their Atlantic defenses to hold the Allies as close to the sea as possible. The Allied commanders realized that behind the reinforced Atlantic defenses the Germans were preparing for a desperate last-ditch stand that might throw the invasion forces back into the sea.

General Eisenhower was soon aware that considerable planning and preparing for OVERLORD remained to be done. Three days after he arrived in London he wrote to General Marshall:

> It is obvious that strong and positive action is needed here in several directions. The location of various headquarters, the exact pattern of command, the tactics of the assault, and the strength in units and equipment, are all questions that have not been definitely settled. The most important of all these questions is that of increasing the strength of the initial assault wave in OVERLORD.

Now that a commander had been charged with the responsibility for ensuring the success of OVERLORD, an operation that was no longer merely a contingency, the burden of American staff work shifted from Washington to London. For the next few months General Eisenhower and his staff were engrossed in completing the infinite number of preparations essential to the success of the invasion. The Combined Chiefs of Staff relied heavily on the judgment of General Eisenhower and his staff and made decisions on organizational, logistical, and tactical questions as they were presented. Certainly the large role in strategic and operational planning in coalition warfare that the overseas commanders and large theater headquarters played was well illustrated early in 1944 during the preparations for OVERLORD.

Nevertheless, General Marshall and his planning staff in Washington closely followed the planning and final preparations for OVERLORD. This operation was the climax of many weary months of planning, organizing, training, equipping, and husbanding the citizen Army. With the undertaking in General Eisenhower's hands, the War Department staff began to give more attention to such related problems as logistical preparations and politico-military terms on which the war might be concluded. The Washington planners endeavored to anticipate General Eisenhower's requirements and to support his actions through visits to London and conferences with him and his staff representatives in London and Washington.

General Marshall offered suggestions and counsel to General Eisenhower, sometimes by invitation, other times on his own initiative, although final decisions were left to the judgment of the Commander. General Marshall also endeavored to strengthen the Supreme Commander's position in relation to his superiors and his subordinates. He was a firm believer in giving the responsible commander wide latitude and in offering him his choice of outstanding corps and division commanders. As a result there was a heavy flow of transatlantic correspondence to assign the most competent personnel available for OVERLORD organizations.

The Manpower Problem

During the SEXTANT Conference, the Joint Logistics Committee had estimated that there would be a serious shortage of service troops during 1944 for the war against Japan, and also a shortage of men for the B-29 program. It suggested that the Army troop basis be revised to anticipate those shortages and that the United States take a calculated risk and eliminate the 15 infantry divisions that were to be activated in 1944. That would leave the Army with 90 divisions—43 for Europe, 7 for North Africa, 22 for the Pacific, and 18 for the continental reserve. If necessary, service troops could be organized from the 18 reserve divisions. The War Department Strategy Section substantiated that estimate in December 1943, although the allocation was slightly different.

The activation of the 15 divisions was deferred, but as a result of the continuing scarcity of service troops, General Marshall called a conference of theater G-4s (supply and logistics staff officers) to Washington in late January to consider the problem. The Army was trying desperately to stay within the 7,700,000 ceiling and to meet needs from within by rigid economy and adjustment. In early February General Marshall discussed the whole Army personnel problem with the JCS. He pointed out that the ground forces were short about 87,000 to 97,000 troops and were forced to take men from other divisions to fill those going overseas. Economies had resulted in a saving of 100,000 men, but the B-29 program had absorbed this saving. There was a deficiency of 100,000 service troops for OVERLORD, ANVIL, and western Pacific operations, and a large number of tactical units was being used to help in the housekeeping of training establishments in the United States in order to release service forces for overseas duty. General Marshall estimated that replacements and rotation fillers, added to induction shortages and ground force and service deficiencies, made the current deficit between 350,000 and 400,000 men.

General Marshall decided that the time had arrived for taking drastic measures. On Feb. 10 he cut back the Army Specialized Training Program that had been established to educate some of its more intelligent men in colleges to 30,000 men, thus releasing 120,000 men for distribution mainly to ground and service forces. Later in the month he was able to get presidential pressure on the War Manpower Commission and the Selective Service to review occupational deferments and to provide the manpower required by the armed services. Most of the induction backlog was made up by spring.

Of all the calculated risks taken by General Marshall and his staff in preparing for OVERLORD, the greatest gamble was the decision to hold to the 90-division troop basis. But even on the eve of OVERLORD some uneasy doubts about the gamble were held in high Washington military circles. Secretary of War Henry L. Stimson, a long-time advocate of the cross-Channel operation, raised the issue with General Marshall. He argued that against an estimated 56 German divisions that were to defend France, the United States would have barely more than an equal number available for the offensive by the end of summer. Current Army calculations, both in the European theater and the United States, seemed to the Secretary "to shave the line of sufficiency rather narrowly instead of aiming at massive abundance." When all OVERLORD divisions had left the United States, only 14 uncommitted divisions would remain, and those would be practically the only reserve for operations in France. The British had no reserve divisions, and the estimated German reserve of 11 divisions was almost as large as the American reserve. Secretary Stimson feared that a stalemate might develop in November when weather conditions on the Continent would reduce the ability to maneuver. "Furthermore, the Russians are already reaching boundary lines where they conceivably might stop with their ground strategic objective of national defense satisfied by the eviction of the invader and the gaining back of all they had lost, plus the Baltic States." To forestall a stalemate, he asked if new manpower legislation should not be sought before the November elections, and should not new divisions be activated now by the War Department?

Just three weeks before OVERLORD was launched General Marshall replied to Secretary Stimson. Although he agreed that everything possible must be done to preclude a stalemate, he did not concur with either the analysis or the conclusion. He wrote, "We are about to invade the Continent and have staked our success on our air superiority, on Soviet numerical preponderance, and on the high quality of our ground combat units." General Marshall felt that "the air arm should be our most effective weapon in bringing home to the German people and the German Army the futility of continued resistance." Further, he declared, "Our equipment, high standard of training, and freshness should give us a superiority which the enemy cannot meet and which we could not achieve by resorting to a matching of numerical strength." Following conversations between Ambassador W. Averell Harriman and Premier Joseph Stalin, General Marshall believed that the Soviets would continue their current efforts until Germany was defeated. He also informed the Secretary that the most difficult factor would be the comparatively slow rate of American buildup that would result from purely logistical limitations. If, however, a stalemate did occur, then new major strategic decisions would be required. The General concluded, "Considering the matter from all angles and with the realization of the hazards involved, I believe that at the present time no increase should be made in the overall strength of the Army, except as may be necessary to provide replacements."

Obviously General Marshall considered the Allied divisions in the Mediterranean as part of the strategic reserve for the invasion of Europe. As the debate over ANVIL would show, he was anxious to make what he regarded as the surplus U.S. and French divisions in Italy available to support the main effort in France, just as he had earlier believed in withdrawing 7 British and U.S. divisions from the Mediterranean for OVERLORD.

The magnitude of this calculated risk was emphasized by General Marshall's decision to allocate military manpower for the B-29 program for the war against Japan instead of activating more divisions. Whether this bold calculation would be justified by the largely untested U.S. Army divisions remained to be proved.

Debates over ANVIL, OVERLORD,
and Operations in Italy

In the early months of 1944 an Anglo-American debate developed, first concerning ANVIL and OVERLORD and then over ANVIL and operations in Italy. To obtain the necessary landing craft for the OVERLORD assault, the SHAEF staff recommended the abandonment of ANVIL except as a threat. General Eisenhower reported to General Marshall on Jan. 17: ". . . This seems to me to be justified only as a last resort. . . . However, I think the question to be weighed is that of increasing our insurance in obtaining the first foothold on the beaches against the advantages that would accrue from a really successful ANVIL."

Two additional considerations were believed important by General Eisenhower. First, the British and Americans had assured the Soviets at Tehran that ANVIL would be launched. Second, the United States had a considerable investment in the French Army. If ANVIL were not undertaken, a large number of U.S. and French divisions would be wasted in the Mediterranean. General Eisenhower therefore stated that he would explore every possibility for increasing the initial assault force of OVERLORD before he would recommend any substantial weakening of ANVIL. Those views were shared by General Marshall and his staff. To them, ANVIL and OVERLORD were essential parts of the same undertaking.

The planning staffs on both sides of the Atlantic carefully examined the implications and cost of expanding the OVERLORD assault and searched for ways to resolve the problem. By postponing the target date for OVERLORD from May 1 to May 31, an extra month's production of landing craft would become available. The disadvantage of losing one month of good weather for ground operations would be offset by more favorable weather on the Soviet front and an additional month of Allied air operations over Europe. The postponement was agreed to by the JCS and the British Chiefs of Staff.

In February the ANVIL debate was complicated by a new factor. The British had become as much concerned over the additional needs for the campaign in Italy as they were over those for the OVERLORD assault. They were convinced that the war in Italy, which had bogged down, must be resumed vigorously. The American staff in Washington immediately saw the specter of a second front draining resources from OVERLORD. Both Washington and London were concerned by the stalemate in Italy. The Allied push had been halted just above the Volturno and Sangro rivers in December 1943 by a combination of rugged terrain, miserable winter weather, and determined German resistance. At the same time the new Allied command structure in the Mediterranean enabled Churchill to play a more leading role in the conduct of the Italian campaign. He was firmly convinced that a vigorous campaign in Italy in the first half of 1944 could offer the greatest assistance to the cross-Channel invasion, and he was determined to end the stalemate in Italy.

At an Allied commanders' conference in Carthage (Tunis) on Dec. 26, 1943, he had made a decision to launch Operation SHINGLE (an amphibious operation at Anzio). This decision was confirmed at Marrakech on Jan. 7 and 8, 1944. It was hoped that the assault would force the Germans back and leave open the road to Rome. Much to Churchill's delight, President Roosevelt agreed to a temporary delay in the departure of 56 landing craft scheduled for OVERLORD on condition that OVERLORD would not be delayed. General Marshall also authorized a delay in the transfer of the 504th U.S. Parachute Regimental Combat Team, one medium bombardment group, two fighter groups, and two service groups until ten days after the SHINGLE D-day.

The U.S. VI Corps made a successful landing at Anzio on Jan. 22, 1944, but the U.S. Fifth Army was stopped at the Gustav Line and the beachhead at Anzio, which prevented the planned link-up and drive on to Rome. Churchill commented on the operation: "I had hoped that we were hurling a wildcat on the shore, but all we got was a stranded whale." Moreover, the Anzio assault removed the uncertainty of the German High Command over Allied intentions. After the landings, German fears of a Balkan invasion were dispelled because they realized that the Allies had their hands full in Italy. By early February the British concluded that the Germans intended to fight it out in central Italy; that some of the troops designated for ANVIL and landing craft for one division for end runs should be set aside for the Italian campaign, and that the war in Italy must be conducted forcefully.

Although General Marshall did not oppose an Allied advance to just north of Rome, he was convinced that planning and preparations for ANVIL should continue. If by April the Allies were not securely established north of Rome, then ANVIL would have to be abandoned. But if ANVIL were called off immediately, there would be no possibility of launching it in the spring, even though conditions were favorable.

General Eisenhower found himself in a difficult position between the divergent views of the British and the War Department. Although agreeing with the War Department's estimate of the importance of ANVIL, he was responsible for the success of OVERLORD, and the planning problems were beginning to make ANVIL less practicable. General Marshall considered ANVIL an important under-taking and he was surprised to find the Americans strongly supporting the Mediterranean project. In a letter to General Eisenhower of Feb. 7 he wrote: "Judging from the discussions and differences of opinion at the present time the British and American Chiefs of Staff seem to have completely reversed themselves and we have become Mediterraneanites and they heavily pro-OVERLORD."

The landing craft shortage was making Anglo-American agreement on operations difficult. General Marshall added, "Our difficulties in reaching a decision have been complicated by a battle of numbers, that is, a failure to reach a common ground as to what would be the actual facilities." The Washington planners had agreed that there was sufficient lift for a 7-division assault for OVERLORD and a 2-division ANVIL assault. But the British planners in London, or General Sir Bernard L. Montgomery, who was in charge of the assault phase of OVERLORD—General Marshall did not know which—disagreed with those figures. If General Eisenhower agreed with the British, OVERLORD would have to be abandoned and, in that case, General Eisenhower would lose the support of 8 or 9 divisions fighting the enemy. Could he afford that loss in view of a possible French uprising against the Germans in Southern France? In concluding his Feb. 7 letter, General Marshall wrote, "I will use my influence here to agree with your desires. I merely wish to be certain that localitis is not developing and that the pressures on you have not warped your judgment."

Stung by General Marshall's reference to "localitis," General Eisenhower replied promptly, recounting his position on OVERLORD and ANVIL from the beginning. Since arriving in London he had been trying to preserve ANVIL by all means possible, yet at the same time trying to find the necessary strength for OVERLORD. He had resisted recommendations to abandon ANVIL and would do so only as a last resort. Between ANVIL and the campaign in Italy, he agreed with the Chief of Staff that ANVIL would be the more desirable supporting operation. But if the Allies could not soon achieve their objectives in Italy, they would be committed to that campaign with nothing to spare for ANVIL. He wrote: ". . . . So far as I am aware, no one here has tried to urge me to present any particular view, nor do I believe that I am particularly affected by localitis. I merely recognize that OVERLORD, which has been supported earnestly for more than two years by the U.S. Chiefs of Staff, represents for the United States and the United Kingdom a crisis in the European War."

Although General Eisenhower's reply reassured General Marshall, the number of landing craft for OVERLORD and ANVIL was still hanging. Soon, however, a mutual understanding was agreed upon. In the "battle of numbers" between Washington and London planners there was a difference of about 14,000 troops out of a total of 176,000 desired for the OVERLORD assault and immediate follow-up, and a difference of 1,000 vehicles out of a total of about 20,000. To resolve the issue, General Marshall proposed that the JCS delegate its authority to General Eisenhower and that a conference be held between him and the British Chiefs of Staff. Those proposals were promptly approved in Washington and London.

The Washington delegation, headed by Major General John E. Hull of the Operations Division, arrived in London on Feb. 12 to serve as adviser to General Eisenhower. As the week-long series of negotiations progressed, the Americans formed definite impressions of the British staff concerning OVERLORD and ANVIL. General Hull reported to the War Department that the British planners thought strongly "that OVERLORD is not only the main show but . . . the only one which would pay us dividends." They saw "no relationship between OVERLORD and ANVIL." As far as the British were concerned, "ANVIL might be an operation in the Marshalls." In a message to the War Department the following day, Colonel George A. Lincoln stated, "As we thought, the local people, except the Supreme Commander, are not impressed with the value of ANVIL."

General Eisenhower, as representative of the JCS, took a flexible position: Planning for ANVIL should be continued until it was obvious that the operation would have to be abandoned. To meet OVERLORD requirements for a strengthened assault and still have enough landing craft for a 2-division ANVIL, General Eisenhower recommended a shipping compromise on Feb. 19. By this time the British Chiefs felt that ANVIL should be completely canceled. The proposed recommendations of shipping allocations would skimp on both operations. Further, the Italian campaign was not developing as expected, and the heavy demands for that struggle made ANVIL more remote. Since the enemy had decided to make a stand south of Rome, it offered an opportunity to bleed the German divisions to the benefit of the Allies. General Montgomery wrote General Eisenhower on Feb. 21: "I recommend very strongly that we now throw the whole weight of our opinion onto the scales against ANVIL. Let us have two really good major campaigns—one in Italy and one in OVERLORD."

The British attitude toward ANVIL caused a sharp reaction in Washington. At a special meeting on Feb. 21, President Roosevelt and the JCS agreed that ANVIL should not be canceled. The President doubted that the Soviets would favor cancellation and felt that the issue should not be raised with them at this time. He directed General Eisenhower to call the attention of the British to the fact that, aside from military considerations, the U.S. and the British were committed to the Soviets and that no move should be made to abandon ANVIL without first taking up the matter with them. Supported by the President and the JCS, General Eisenhower refused to accept General Montgomery's recommendation.

As a result of a compromise agreed to by General Eisenhower and the British Chiefs on Feb. 24, ANVIL was kept alive. Overriding priority over all other Mediterranean operations was given to the Allied campaign in Italy. Subject to that priority, the Allied Commander-in-Chief, Mediterranean, would prepare alternative plans to support OVERLORD. The first alternative would be ANVIL on approximately the date and of the size originally planned (a 2-division assault launched simultaneously with OVERLORD). General Eisenhower's reallocations of shipping and landing craft proposed on Feb. 19 would be put into effect, and the craft were to sail in April. The compromise would be reviewed again on March 20, and if, in light of the Italian campaign, it was decided that ANVIL was impracticable, the lift for more than one division would be withdrawn from the Mediterranean for OVERLORD. That arrangement was approved by the President, the Prime Minister, and the CCS.

Unfortunately the compromise did not resolve the OVERLORD-ANVIL debate. Planning for the OVERLORD assault remained undetermined because of the uncertainty of the number of available landing craft. In the Mediterranean, the C-in-C, concerned over the situation at Anzio, wanted to delay the proposed transfers of shipping—a proposal that was endorsed as strongly by the British Chiefs as it was opposed by the U.S. Chiefs.

As the War Department search for more assault lift continued, Lieutenant General Brehon B. Somervell, U.S. Services of Supply, asked whether the main effort in Europe might not be reinforced at the expense of the Pacific. The answer was negative. General Eisenhower had been given everything in the way of lift he had requested except a small percentage of landing craft, whereas none had been sent to the Pacific for months. Everything out of new production was going to Europe, and landing craft could not be shifted to Europe in time, even if it were agreed upon.

Despite the vigorous and costly Allied attacks on the main front at Cassino in February and early March, the situation in Italy failed to improve. A gap still existed between the main battle line and the bridgehead, and the Allies were unable to start their drive on Rome. When the Mediterranean situation was reviewed on March 20, General Sir Henry M. Wilson, C-in-C, Mediterranean, and the British Chiefs insisted that a simultaneous ANVIL be abandoned. They argued that it would be impossible to withdraw troops from the battle area in Italy or landing craft from the Anzio beachhead in time. Generals Eisenhower and Wilson were now agreed that the landing craft in the Mediterranean should be reduced to a one-division lift. The following day General Eisenhower also concluded to cancel ANVIL as a simultaneous operation with OVERLORD. Those recommendations were approved, and the landing craft in question were ordered to be reallocated to OVERLORD. Firm planning for an expanded cross-Channel assault could now proceed.

Cancellation of the simultaneous ANVIL was a welcome relief in both theaters. Aside from the landing craft issue, ground forces on the Italian fronts were battle-weary, and the two divisions designated for ANVIL were needed at Anzio. The Washington planners realized that it would be difficult, if not impossible, to open another front in the Mediterranean before the Italian campaign was concluded.

One consequence of the expanded OVERLORD was the highlighting of the shortages in the Mediterranean of service troops and replacements. In order to partly offset the shortage of service personnel, the War Department approved a plan to ship the 2d Cavalry Division and other combat units to the Mediterranean and reorganize them into service units. In the meantime, however, General Jacob L. Devers, commander of U.S. troops in the MTO, had already begun to close down supply and administrative installations in North Africa. As General Devers expressed it, "We are trying in every way to roll up our tail as soon as possible."

The debate over ANVIL versus the campaign in Italy was not ended by the decision to cancel a simultaneous ANVIL. The British and U.S. Chiefs were in complete accord that the Anzio beachhead must be joined with the main battle line in Italy. Prolonging the stalemate was not only a threat to the safety of the forces on the beachhead, but could possibly upset the OVERLORD timetable. Once the bridgehead was linked to the Fifth Army front, the major course of action in the Mediterranean would have to be decided. Old differences between the two staffs were rehashed.

The argument became a matter of options. When the link-up was accomplished, the British wanted to continue the Italian campaign—but the Americans wanted to launch ANVIL. The British felt that when an all-out offensive was launched in Italy, it should continue until June; then a final decision could be made, based on the situations in Italy and France. The U.S. Chiefs insisted that when the two fronts in Italy were joined, nothing should interfere with ANVIL. The Americans were willing to divert to the Mediterranean landing craft due to leave for the Pacific in May and June if the British would agree to making plans and preparations for a July 10 2-division ANVIL assault. General Marshall wrote to General Eisenhower, "We will not make this diversion which means a serious delay in the Pacific with the possibility of losing our momentum unless some sizeable operation of the nature of ANVIL is on the books." The JCS considered that the proposed July 10 ANVIL operation should have precedence over reaching Rome, an objective of great importance to the British. The British, however, were unwilling to accept the windfall of landing craft for a firmly scheduled ANVIL.

Behind the American pressure to keep ANVIL alive was the desire to bring the war against Germany to a quick, decisive end with the least possible political involvement. The staff summed it up this way: If we cancel ANVIL completely, the following will be true:

a. We will get into political difficulties with the French.

b. OVERLORD will lose at least ten fighting divisions.

c. Our service forces will continue to support the western Mediterranean.

d. Our divisions and the French divisions will be committed to a costly, unremunerative, inching advance in Italy. The people of both the United States and France may or may not take this indefinitely.

e. Once committed to Italy, we will have our forces pointed towards southeastern Europe and will have the greatest difficulty in preventing their use for occupation forces in Austria, Hungary, and southern Germany.

The War Department was haunted by the large number of Allied combat divisions contained in the Mediterranean, instead of supporting the major offensive pointed at the German heartland.

The debate continued. The British would not agree that preparations for ANVIL should take precedence over continuing the battle in Italy after the bridgehead and main battle line had been joined.

The Prime Minister began to participate in the discussion in early April. He urged that the choice be deferred, stating that the option between Italy and ANVIL would not exist unless the landing craft scheduled for the Pacific were diverted to the Mediterranean. General Marshall replied that if any option were to exist, preparations for ANVIL would have to be started at once. Without a guarantee of a definite ANVIL, the United States would not feel justified in sacrificing the momentum that had been attained in the Pacific and that was so important to shortening the war against Japan. The Prime Minister answered General Marshall: ". . . . The whole of this difficult question only arises out of the absurd shortage of LST's. How it is that the plans of two great empires like Britain and the United States should be so much hamstrung and limited by a hundred or two of these particular vessels will never be understood by history."

To resolve the problem, the British Chiefs proposed a compromise directive for General Wilson that was accepted by the U.S. Chiefs on April 18. Allied resources and strength in the Mediterranean were to be deployed in an all-out offensive in Italy that was to have first priority. Within those terms, plans and preparations could be made for ANVIL or to exploit further the campaign in Italy. Since neither the target date for ANVIL nor additional landing craft were mentioned, ANVIL was deferred indefinitely, and OVERLORD would not have the support of the Southern France assault.

The Allied command in Italy launched a full-scale ground offensive on May 12—Operation DIADEM. The bridgehead and the main battle line were joined and the deadlock in Italy was broken. Moreover, on June 4, two days before the OVERLORD assault was launched, Allied forces captured Rome. Even so, the OVERLORD-ANVIL Italian campaign debate of the early months of 1944 led to no final decision on Mediterranean strategy. It was not until after OVERLORD was launched that the question of Operation ANVIL was conclusively resolved.

Chapter IV

Decline of the CBI Theater

President Roosevelt's decision at SEXTANT to accept the British view that the bulk of Southeast Asia Command's landing craft might be put to better use in OVERLORD and ANVIL necessitated a reassessment of the strategical value of the CBI in relation to the overall war against Japan. Although no disagreement existed between the British and the Americans as to the need of landing craft for the major operations in the primary war, the Americans feared that a transfer of the landing craft would solidify the policy of delay and inaction in Burma to such an extent that it would be impossible to mount any important offensive there. The rapid progress of operations in the Pacific gave indications that any undertaking in Burma would be anticlimactic unless it were executed during 1944. U.S. planners had to deal with the problem of keeping CBI and Pacific operations in phase, as well as the problems of Chinese reluctance to engage large forces in Burma and the British antipathy for jungle warfare.

The President had further complicated the planners' problems on Dec. 5 by offering Generalissimo Chiang Kai-shek the choice of going ahead with land operations in North Burma or waiting until the fall when sufficient resources would be on hand to mount an amphibious operation in the SEAC area. Both the President and Admiral Lord Louis Mountbatten erroneously assumed that SEAC would not have enough landing craft left to stage an amphibious assault larger than a raid until fall. Chiang not only accepted the delay, but on Dec. 9 presented a new set of requirements that he considered necessary to keep China in the war. In addition to a $1,000,000,000 gold loan to support the Chinese economy, he wanted the U.S. and

Chinese air forces in China doubled and the Hump airlift increased to 20,000 tons per month.

The Washington planners were not alarmed over these demands. It was their opinion that although the Generalissimo would resent a failure to carry out the Burma campaign, he felt he was associated with the victors in the war and would not withdraw from his association despite his disappointment over the Burma campaign. President Roosevelt's reply of Dec. 19 reflected that attitude and contained a note of firmness that had been lacking in previous high-level messages. The President stated that the major contribution that could be made to aid China was to open the land supply route to China, and he hoped that the Generalissimo would cooperate by authorizing the use of his Yunnan forces in North Burma. Additional transport planes were en route to CBI that should provide 12,000 tons a month over the Hump, provided there was no interference by the Japanese. General Chennault's air forces could not be expanded until logistical problems were solved. Finally, the President added that the request for the billion-dollar loan had been turned over to the Treasury Department for study.

The Generalissimo did not agree with the President's suggestion to employ his Yunnan forces in North Burma, but he would agree to use the Ledo Chinese forces in the campaign. He felt that their employment would not have an adverse effect on the situation in China.

In the meantime Lord Mountbatten had increased the strength of his amphibious force from 20,000 to 30,000 troops, which were supported by an even larger number of service troops. In the theater, plans were prepared for an amphibious assault against Akyab to satisfy the Generalissimo's insistence upon simultaneous land and sea operations. On the War Department's recommendation the President again urged Chiang Kai-shek to commit his Yunnan troops, pointing out that the urgent need of Hump resources precluded using them for any undertaking that would not yield results in the near future. The President's implied threat to Yunnan allocations if those troops were to remain inactive was the first indication of his impatience with a continuation of the status quo.

The Generalissimo adhered to his conditions for employing the Yunnan troops, with the result that the British Chiefs of Staff acted unilaterally to dispense with all amphibious operations in SEAC during the current dry season. Early in January 1944 they ordered Lord Mountbatten to return his three remaining landing craft (tanks) to the Mediterranean. The British action postponed any amphibious assault until fall. The U.S. Chiefs accepted the British action because amphibious operations in the Bay of Bengal would be dangerous during the coming monsoon season.

With action in Burma reduced to limited ground offensives, the Washington, London, and theater planners began in January 1944 to examine the possible roles of China and SEAC in the overall strategic concept. The SEAC theater planners favored building up the air route and supporting General Chennault and the B-29 program while conducting minor operations in Burma and preparing for a campaign against the Malaya–Netherlands East Indies barrier, followed by an advance northward. The Ledo Road would be constructed as far as Myitkyina to support new air ferry operations. Lord Mountbatten proposed to send a mission to Washington and London to present the plans to the CCS. General Joseph W. Stilwell, however, was diametrically opposed to this shift of strategy that would result in abandoning large-scale operations in Burma. He therefore sent a U.S. mission to Washington to present his views to the JCS. Although General Stilwell, as commanding general of U.S. forces in CBI, was authorized to send a delegation to the War Department, Lord Mountbatten felt that, as Deputy Commander, SEAC, General Stilwell was undercutting his commanding general.

For the War Department, any change in strategy for SEAC raised a problem of the future role of China, since all U.S. manpower and resources in CBI were there to support SEAC insofar as it, in turn, tried to relieve China. Few illusions were held in the War Department in January 1944 about the value of China in the war against Japan. U.S. intelligence estimates indicated that China had little desire to do any actual fighting, although it might engage in limited operations to gain a seat at the peace table. The estimates concluded that China's value would be to contain Japanese divisions in China and provide air bases for Allied aircraft.

The Strategy Section, OPD, examined the question of China's military value and reported: "The only effective contributory effort toward the defeat of Japan from the China theater in 1945–46 will be limited air support of the main effort in the Pacific area from bases now securely in our possession." It estimated that the Chinese Army could not be trained and equipped until too late to support the Pacific drive. It was therefore recommended that air strength in China be built up to provide support for the Pacific advance, and that Chinese ground forces not be equipped any further until it was decided whether ground operations would actually accelerate the defeat of Japan.

That recommendation drew some protests within the War Department. In defending the estimate it was stated that ". . . China's past and present contribution to the war against Japan is recognized, as well as the necessity for maintaining China as a base. However, it is considered that only an unexpected catastrophe will cause her collapse. Our most practical recourse now to prevent such a collapse, as well as to provide support from that area for Pacific operations, is to build up air strength."

Major General John E. Hull, OPD, observed, "In some respects as regards China we have a bear by the tail. It is difficult to hold on but we cannot let loose." He pointed out that if the United States desired to use China as an air base and to keep the Japanese divisions in China pinned down, it would have to go on supporting China. The land route to China would not be ready in time to assist U.S. Pacific operations, nor would the Chinese army be able to take a port on the China coast. On the other hand, the United States could not take anything away from CBI without interfering with the flow of supplies into China necessary to assure the accomplishment of the two vital purposes. In General Hull's opinion, the War Department should screen all requests from CBI that did not benefit those two main projects. Thus it was becoming evident that the U.S. investment in CBI had reached a point at which, although it had to be sustained for political and psychological reasons, it had become militarily and economically a losing proposition. From the grandiose schemes for utilizing China's manpower, to the realization that the United States could not pull out of China even if it wanted to, was a marked change in military thinking. From now on, planning could be conducted on a more realistic basis, and China's role would become less and less important.

SEAC's Future

Early in February 1944 a series of conferences was held in Washington, attended by Army and Navy staff personnel and General Stilwell's representatives. SEAC strategy matters discussed included long-range penetration groups, the Yunnan and Ledo Chinese forces, and the logistics problems in CBI. General Stilwell's views on North Burma operations and the Hump airlift buildup strengthened the position of the Army planners. Shortly after the meetings concluded, General Marshall briefed the President on the American and British positions on future operations in SEAC and submitted the briefs prepared by Lord Mountbatten and General Stilwell.

Under the Mountbatten concept, overland communication with

China would not be reestablished within any reasonable time under the present circumstances. The quickest way of making contact with China would be to open a port on the China coast, and if forces were made available after Germany's collapse, then SEAC's greatest contribution could be an operation against Sumatra, which he believed could be carried out in October or November 1944.

General Stilwell rejected the concept for a number of reasons. There was no certainty that operations along the Netherlands East Indies–China Seas route would open a port in China more quickly than those along the Burma-Yunnan road, and the former would require a frontal assault using large amphibious resources if Sumatra were to be attacked. Even granted that Sumatra were taken, the Japanese blockade of China would still be in effect, and the difficulties of a campaign in the NEI were largely unknown. General Stilwell also pointed out that the SEAC plan was based on the assumption that Germany would be defeated at an early date and that that was a highly uncertain factor. He felt that the best way for SEAC to help the war effort would be to use its available resources at once to defeat the enemy.

General Stilwell's concept agreed with the War Department's ideas. Consequently General Marshall urged the British Chiefs to instruct Lord Mountbatten to conduct the war in North Burma with the resources available, with Myitkyina as the first objective of the current dry season. He also prepared a message that President Roosevelt dispatched to Churchill in regard to SEAC: "I am gravely concerned over the recent trends in strategy that favor an operation toward Sumatra and Malaya in the future rather than to face the immediate obstacles that confront us in Burma. I fail to see how an operation against Sumatra and Malaya, requiring tremendous resources and forces, can possibly be mounted until after the conclusion of the war in Europe. Lucrative as a successful CULVERIN [operation toward Sumatra] might be, there appears much more to be gained by employing all the resources we now have available in an all-out drive into upper Burma so that we can build our air strength in China and insure the essential support for our westward advance to the Formosa-China-Luzon area."

Churchill asked the President to wait until General Albert C. Wedemeyer and other members of the SEAC mission arrived in Washington and presented Lord Mountbatten's views before he made up his mind. For many months the President and his planners had favored operations in Burma as opposed to Sumatra. The President now believed that any southern Burma or Sumatra operation would be "shots in the dark" and would be far less important than those planned for China. When the State Department endorsed the North Burma campaign, it was the first time in the Far Eastern war that the United States presented a united front to the British and the Chinese.

British resentment over General Stilwell's alleged role in hardening the U.S. attitude resulted in some unfavorable publicity. General Marshall therefore instructed General Stilwell to straighten out the misunderstanding with Lord Mountbatten. He urged General Stilwell to seek a "working basis that is not complicated by suspicions and stiffness that makes Allied procedure unworkable." He pointed out that "This is a matter of great importance not merely to your theater but in its effect on combined operations all over the world which depend upon our relationship with the British high officials."

The difficulty suddenly became academic when the Japanese launched an attack in mid-March that threatened to capture the Imphal Plain on the central Burma front and to cut the Assam line of communications. Confronted by that attack, SEAC was compelled to give its attention to halting the enemy's campaign. As a result, SEAC's future awaited the outcome of the Japanese undertaking. While Japanese forces were fighting on the Imphal front and General Stilwell's Chinese forces advanced toward Myitkyina, the War Department renewed its efforts to get Chiang Kai-shek to use his Yunnan forces to relieve the enemy pressure. However, he still held out those troops in return for an amphibious operation in the south, although he permitted his Ledo force to be reinforced by troops flown in from Yunnan.

The situation in the Imphal Plain became more precarious in April, causing President Roosevelt to make a final effort to persuade Chiang to move Yunnan troops into Burma. The appeal was accompanied by a threat that unless he did so, supplies to those troops would be stopped. Either that warning or the realization that further delay might later be used against China had the desired effect, and four Yunnan divisions were moved into Burma in mid-April.

Although not as originally conceived, the three-pronged assault on North Burma was finally underway. But at that point the War Department was wondering just what the capture of North Burma, or even all of Burma, might mean. It was an accepted fact that China had to be kept in the war, and the Allies could achieve this more easily with the Burma Road opened. However, with the expansion of the Hump airlift, the Burma Road would be helpful but not absolutely essential. The buildup of U.S. Army Air Forces in China to support the Pacific drive was important provided it could be phased into the Pacific operations.

The War Department's interest in Burma operations was diminishing. If North Burma could be held south of Myitkyina, it would provide the necessary security for the North Burma Road, the Air Transport Command, and the India-to-China pipeline. There was therefore little desire to conquer all Burma, particularly since U.S. combat troops would probably have to be committed, and General Marshall had given no indication of using combat forces in CBI except for a long-range penetration group.

The JCS then decided that Lord Mountbatten should be instructed by the CCS to proceed vigorously with operations in North Burma, even during the monsoon, to build up the air route and lay the pipeline. The British were also informed that four groups of transport aircraft could be sent to SEAC beginning in June. The need for a directive to Lord Mountbatten was urged by General Stilwell, who believed that the Generalissimo had given his commanders an order to slow down. In May General Stilwell was made responsible, by a JCS directive, for air support from China against Formosa, the Ryukyus, the Philippines, and the China coast before and during the advance on Formosa in February 1945. He was also instructed to provide indirect support to the Mindanao landings in November if it could be performed without prejudicing his current operations. Although the JCS realized that air support of future Pacific operations from China would result in a curtailment of supplies to ground forces in China, they nevertheless directed that stockpiling for air support operations begin immediately.

The JCS directive marked the beginning of a new U.S. military policy respecting CBI and was indicative of the realistic attitude in Washington. No longer would General Stilwell's primary mission be the paper objectives of helping the British in Burma and improving the combat efficiency of the Chinese troops. The opening of the Burma Road was still considered desirable, mainly as a safety factor, because a setback in the Pacific timetable might permit the Burma–China Road undertaking to be brought into phase again. The equipment for building and utilizing the Ledo and Burma roads would not be available in time for the Pacific operations—unless projected plans failed to materialize, in which case the Army planners wanted to be able to use the land route. On June 3 the CCS sent a directive to Lord Mountbatten that substantially followed the U.S. recommendations. Operations in North Burma were to be conducted with those resources available in or already allocated to SEAC. That restriction on resources confirmed General Marshall's judgment of the role of the CBI theater.

In the six-month period after SEXTANT, certain factors were emerging out of the labyrinth of discussions and negotiations on strategy and operations in the Asiatic theater. The theater was to be subordinate to, and dependent upon, the main advance in the Pacific. The use of Chinese troops in large-scale operations was eliminated. Since China had to be kept in the war and supported politically, and since it was suitable as a base for air operations, future emphasis would be placed solely on the development of air forces, unless a delay in the Pacific advance permitted time to utilize Chinese manpower. SEAC's primary task would be to strengthen and develop the air route to China, since the most feasible means of aiding the main effort in the war against Japan was through air operations.

The B-29 Offensive

In CBI the U.S. air commander, Major General George E. Stratemeyer, had a status similar to that of General Stilwell. Part of General Stratemeyer's command, the Tenth Air Force, had been integrated with the RAF in India in December and was operating under Lord Mountbatten. Another part of it, the Fourteenth Air Force, was in China and was technically under the command of the Generalissimo as the theater commander. Further, although the India-China wing of the Air Transport Command received its tonnage assignments from General Stratemeyer, operational control actually was exercised from Washington. When the B-29s arrived in the theater in the spring, the administration and control of air organizations was further complicated. The imposition of command echelons on top of one another resulted in divided responsibilities, and crossing lines of authority caused confusion, particularly during a crisis when demands came from all sides at once. Presumably General Stilwell was the focal point of control and coordination for all air activity but, having assumed personal direction of the advance of the Chinese Ledo forces in North Burma in late 1943, he was frequently out of touch with his own headquarters and with the general situation. As a result, in emergencies when central control and direction were necessary, tactical needs of the emergency frequently overshadowed long-range strategic requirements.

Another problem in CBI was the competition among subordinate commands for manpower and equipment. The introduction of B-29 units into the theater intensified the rivalry, since the bomber program would affect all other theater projects. The Army Air Forces had to secure an increase in their troop basis allotment to man the B-29 organizations, and to transport the first B-29 units (less flight echelons) a ship had to be taken off the U.K. run, airfields had to be built, and facilities constructed for the personnel and the aircraft in both India and China. That requirement drew service and engineer troops from such projects as the Ledo Road. In order to protect the new long-range bombers from Japanese air attacks, fighter aircraft were brought in to defend the airfields in China, and the Tenth Air Force and RAF units were directed to protect the Calcutta airfields. President Roosevelt had promised the Generalissimo fighter protection for the Cheng-tu bases, so in January 1944 two fighter, one medium bomber group (less aircraft), and two service groups were ordered transferred from North Africa.

General Eisenhower, who was concerned over the requirements for ANVIL, immediately protested the transfer of the AAF organizations and asked for reconsideration. His objections were overruled by General Marshall, who directed that the transfer be made by Feb. 15. The Army also persuaded the Navy to transport 100 P-47 fighter aircraft from the Mediterranean to CBI by diverting two escort carriers from the Atlantic-Mediterranean run. The aircraft were scheduled to arrive in CBI in mid-March. Although that would deprive the Atlantic convoys of the protection by the two carriers for more than two months, it would expedite the B-29 offensive.

The Prime Minister was also concerned over the transfer of the AAF fighter groups. In February he asked President Roosevelt to cancel the transfer, pointing out that he had given up his Aegean projects and released eight fighter squadrons for OVERLORD. He stated that other fighter units were scheduled to be sent to the U.K. for OVERLORD but that they would probably have to remain in the MTO. Therefore, despite its priority, OVERLORD would not have that fighter protection. The President replied stating that the cross-Channel assault would have adequate fighter support, and that if aid to Turkey were abandoned, the Mediterranean could even spare additional air units for OVERLORD.

It was soon obvious in CBI that the operation of the fighter groups from bases at Cheng-tu would mean an additional demand on the Hump airlift tonnage. In December 1943 the tonnage lift exceeded the 10,000 monthly figure for the first time (19,450 tons). In January 1944 another gain was achieved when 14,472 tons were flown in. That figure was not exceeded until June. During the spring of 1944 the Japanese assault in the Imphal region caused a critical shortage of gasoline that held down flying operations. Following their arrival in April, B-29's were temporarily used to transport supplies into the forward areas. To remove the bottleneck in the Assam line of communications, the United States urged the British to militarize the Calcutta-Assam communications line. With the Prime Minister's approval, U.S. manpower and equipment were employed to assist the British in that work. The heavy consumption of gasoline by the B-29's was largely responsible for the gasoline shortage, although more than 10,000 tons were flown to Cheng-tu by ATC for the B-29's during February to September 1944.

Initially the B-29 offensive had been conceived for operations from Chinese bases as a morale factor for the Chinese, and because it was believed that bases in China would be available long before bases in the Pacific would be captured and suitable for operations. By early 1944 the Army planners began to have some doubts as to the employment of the B-29's from China because of the complex logistics problems. They suggested that the first eight groups be based in the Southwest Pacific area to strike at enemy-held oil targets in the Netherlands East Indies. The Navy supported the Army planners and urged that the majority of the B-29's be located in the SWPA and only one group be sent to China.

General H. H. Arnold, Commander, Army Air Forces, however, defended the original concept because more bombs could be carried from China bases against Japanese targets, and more Japanese shipping was within range from China bases. In March General Douglas MacArthur, Supreme Commander, SWPA, requested that a group of B-29's be based at Darwin, Australia, to bomb the NEI oil centers. General Marshall advised him that some of these objectives would be attacked by long-range bombers from Ceylon, and that he could attack others with his assigned B-29's from bases in the SWPA.

In April the JCS decided to base four B-29 groups in the Marianas Islands with a target of Sept. 30 for initiating operations. The move was intended to effect a saving in the number of fields, facilities, and service troops needed in the China-India area. But with so many construction programs in progress, not enough service troops were available. Building roads, bridges, airfields, laying pipelines, running railroads, and providing logistic support for U.S. troops and some Chinese forces took a heavy toll of service troops. The War Department was unable to relieve the shortage, which existed throughout the Pacific. Realizing that some adjustment had to be made between the construction planned and the manpower available to do the work, the War Department prepared a list of projects by priority and sent it to the theater. Top priority went to increasing the Hump airlift to 20,000 tons a month; second went to the pipeline construction from Calcutta to Kunming; third to road construction from Ledo to Myitkyina, and on to Kunming if practicable, and finally to a pipeline between Kunming and Tu-shan in east China.

Since a stockpile of about 60,000 tons was required in China to support the B-29 offensive scheduled for early 1945, it was obvious that the Hump tonnage, which dropped to 11,000 tons in March, had to be increased to 20,000 tons. General Arnold estimated that 60,000 tons could be accumulated in time by stockpiling 5,000 tons a month, commencing in April. Until the Hump lift reached 20,000 tons, however, such an accumulation would be impossible in view of the numerous diversions that continued to occur. In July, more than 25,000 tons were delivered to China, and subsequent deliveries continued to rise.

Command of the long-range B-29 bombers presented a new problem. Initially, General Stilwell, under the JCS, would have direct command and control, using Tenth and Fourteenth Air Force facilities. The JCS issued him a directive specifying priority targets. The directive also made him responsible for the defense of B-29 bases in China and Lord Mountbatten responsible for those in SEAC.

The growing interest of the Generalissimo and Lord Mountbatten in the command of aircraft that would be operating through or from their theaters made the initial arrangement temporary. The Army Air Forces was also interested in the problem and in April proposed that since the B-29's would be operating from several theaters and would be transferred wherever needed, General Arnold should be appointed commander of a new air force equipped with B-29's. The mobility gained would permit the planes to be used economically where they could be most useful. Further, it would remove the command problem from the purview of both the Generalissimo and Lord Mountbatten. The concept was similar to that advocated by the Army for the Anti-Submarine Command to become the Tenth Fleet under Admiral Ernest J. King, Chief of Naval Operations in 1943. Despite some objection, the JCS approved the AAF proposal. General Arnold was made the executive agent of the JCS in carrying out their decisions regarding deployments, missions, and targets. Theater commanders were authorized to use B-29's in emergencies and were made responsible for the bomber bases in their areas. On April 4, 1944, the Twentieth Air Force came into existence.

Chiang Kai-shek was personally informed by the President of the need to have central command and control, but the British were not so easily pacified. They made several attempts to bring the control under the CCS, but the JCS replied that when the British were prepared to engage actively in very long-range bombing operations, the matter might be opened for reconsideration.

The B-29's made their first bombing strike against targets in Bangkok as the Allied forces invaded France during the first week of June. It marked the initiation of a threat to the Japanese Inner Zone, which heretofore had been out of range of land-based bombers and had been subject only to nuisance raids from carriers.

The Shortage of Air Transport Aircraft

The eruption of savage fighting along the Central India–Burma frontier initiated a new kind of warfare built around the use of transport aircraft. The use of aircraft for transportation and supply purposes began in 1941 when the British airlifted a battalion of troops from India to Iraq. The Americans first used this technique in the Burma campaign in 1942. During the fall of 1943, air transport squadrons were used in connection with Brigadier Orde C. Wingate's long-range penetration groups and the American jungle warfare forces in Burma. General Arnold's efforts during SEXTANT to find thirty-five C-47 aircraft for SEAC emphasized the importance attached to the great need for troop carrier and cargo planes in the Burma operations.

In CBI, transport-type aircraft were assigned to squadrons of the Tenth Air Force under General Stratemeyer's command and the Air Transport Command, which was controlled from Washington. In January, as the British forces moved along the Arakan coast, the Japanese attempted to cut them off, but they were supplied by air transport planes. Lord Mountbatten borrowed twenty-five aircraft from ATC when the Japanese threat became critical. The Japanese were beaten back and forced to withdraw during February.

When the Japanese attack on the Imphal Plain developed, Lord Mountbatten again asked ATC to help supply his cut-off units. There was even more justification now because, since March 5, Brigadier Wingate's long-range groups had been dropped behind the Japanese lines and were also entirely dependent on air supply. To meet the crisis and provide for future emergencies, Lord Mountbatten requested blanket authority to divert transport aircraft from the Hump without reference to the CCS. This was refused, but the JCS agreed to authorize the temporary diversion of planes from the Hump. The JCS position was that Lord Mountbatten's normal transport requirements were a British concern, whereas all U.S. operations in China were dependent upon the Hump and would suffer from diversions.

As the conflict on the Imphal front increased in intensity, Lord Mountbatten concluded that if he could keep the twenty C-46's borrowed from the Hump and obtain seventy additional C-47's to drop reinforcements to the besieged units and Brigadier Wingate's forces, he could turn the tide. The JCS gave him permission to keep the C-46's, but the British could not provide the seventy C-47's and asked that Lord Mountbatten be allowed to divert them from the Hump. Messages were exchanged between SEAC, Washington, and London with the result that the British agreed to divert an RAF squadron of fifteen C-47-type aircraft from the Mediterranean and to provide thirty-two C-47's from the U.K. The United States agreed to send a troop carrier group (sixty-four C-47's) from the Mediterranean for thirty days' service and to allow Lord Mountbatten to divert thirteen C-47's from the Hump if that proved necessary. This fast action to more than fulfill Lord Mountbatten's request enabled SEAC to carry out its plans and relieve a desperate situation.

The quick response of the CCS to Lord Mountbatten's plea enabled him to refrain from requesting the thirteen C-47's from the Hump and to release some of the C-46's he had borrowed earlier. But since he had to air-supply four Yunnan Chinese divisions that had moved into Burma in April, he wished to retain the seventy-nine C-47's from the Mediterranean. Despite the protests of General Wilson, he was authorized to keep the aircraft until June 15 or until replaced by planes from the United States, whichever was sooner. Although General Stilwell and his forces were locked in conflict at Myitkyina in June 1944, Japanese troops were withdrawing from the Imphal sector as the beleaguered Allied troops turned the tide of battle.

The status of CBI's future was not resolved by SEXTANT decisions; but at the conference the Generalissimo's stubbornness, the British indifference, and the President's attitude were a turning point. Time had overtaken the theater, and its primary purpose now was to support the main Pacific advance. SEAC's first priority was the buildup of the Hump airlift; its second was clearing North Burma of the enemy. China was valuable only for air bases, and already plans had been made to base the bulk of the B-29's in the Marianas, where logistics would not be so difficult.

As the B-29's arrived at air bases in eastern China, they presented a serious threat to the Japanese homeland. The Japanese reacted with a drive that began in April and achieved large proportions in May as it advanced into East China. Even if the Japanese were successful, however, in capturing the air bases and eliminating air support for the Pacific drive from CBI, it would result only in a delay because the Allies no longer considered the CBI theater essential to the defeat of Japan.

Chapter V

Secondary War in the Pacific

The war in the Pacific had been maintained as an American preserve primarily on the grounds that the United States was contributing the bulk of the manpower and resources to fight the Japanese. To retain that freedom of action in the Pacific, the Joint Strategic Survey Committee had pressed the JCS at SEXTANT to establish the priority of the Central Pacific advance over all other Pacific operations. The JSSC called attention to the principal weakness in the new U.S. policy of flexibility:

> The history of our discussions with the British concerning the strategic concept for Europe clearly demonstrates the continuous difficulties which arise when the primacy of the operations in one part of a theater is not clearly set forth and accepted but remains the subject of debate, whenever operations are being considered in another part of the same theater. It is most desirable that we should profit by this experience and have no questions in our own minds as to where the primary effort is to be made in the Pacific.

Although the SEXTANT conference merely confirmed U.S. plans for the Pacific, the decision to undertake OVERLORD ultimately affected every theater of operations. The high-level British-American discussions theretofore had been primarily concerned with planning Mediterranean-European operations and an examination of strategy in SEAC. Even at lower planning echelons few combined efforts had been considered for the war in the Pacific. Now, however, with OVERLORD definitely on the books, Mediterranean operations restricted, and slow progress in SEAC, it could be expected that the

British would become interested in the Pacific island-hopping warfare, which was at last gaining momentum. Although recapture of the Gilbert and Solomon islands, former Empire possessions, was not of vital strategic or economic importance to the British, as the American advance progressed, the retaking of Hong Kong and Singapore would be of special interest to them.

The U.S. Chiefs had not yet decided on future strategy in the Pacific and, at least until then, they did not wish to have the British participate in the Pacific planning. The desire for shortcuts and fast results, the presence of strong personalities in the theater, and the uncertainties of enemy reaction favored a one-two punch advance that would keep the enemy off balance and retain the strategic initiative over the development of a single primary route of advance.

In the immedate post-SEXTANT period, several events occurred that gave the U.S. planners time to study the problem. The first was a difference between the Prime Minister and his Chiefs of Staff on the role of Great Britain in the war against Japan. Churchill was convinced that the British should make the main effort in the Indian Ocean area, with Malaya and the Netherlands East Indies as the goal. The British Chiefs argued that if British forces were to play an important role, they must be based on Australia and operate on General MacArthur's left flank in the Pacific. The difference delayed British entry into the American preserve.

Early in 1944 the British decided to send a naval task force to Australia to operate under General MacArthur. Since he was extremely anxious to increase his naval strength, it was feared that he might overrule U.S. naval objectives, and the British would thereby gain a wedge in Pacific war operations. In February the Japanese inadvertently helped the Americans out of that predicament by moving their major fleet units to Singapore, where they would be closer to fuel supplies and temporarily out of range of U.S. naval and army air forces. That move altered the naval situation in the Indian Ocean and for the time being shelved the project to transfer British warships to the Pacific.

In March the President was asked by the Prime Minister if the U.S. Fleet needed British assistance in the Pacific. He explained that if the British could keep Japanese naval units pinned down at Singapore, the U.S. Fleet would have a clear field in the Pacific. The President assured him that the United States could manage at least until the summer of 1945, which postponed any immediate need to resolve the problem of combined planning in the Pacific.

The American planners were under no misapprehension that this was the end of the British effort and, despite the advantage of a British naval task force in the SWPA, it was feared that combined planning might slow down the increasing war tempo. It was decided that to forestall further efforts the U.S. Chiefs should determine post-Formosa operations and present the British with an accomplished fact. In the spring of 1944 the British planners desired to know what British forces would be required, after the defeat of Germany, to defeat the Japanese. The Americans realized that a rationalization of the U.S. unilateral position would result in endless discussions. The U.S. planners therefore elected to delay any combined planning meetings until the U.S. Chiefs had reached a decision.

On the eve of OVERLORD it was learned that the British Chiefs planned to raise the Pacific problem with the JCS when they came to London for the invasion in order to determine whether India or Australia should be built up as a base for British operations. The report from London stated that the British were not serious about the proposal but intended to use it to try to commit the Prime Minister to the Pacific and permit an Australian buildup. Just how much longer the Americans could avoid a showdown over British participation in the Pacific in the face of mounting high-level British interest was problematical.

Decisions and Options

The U.S. policy of flexibility in the Pacific had the advantage of the element of surprise and permitted the transfer of forces from one axis to another. Its main weakness was the fact that the long-range decisions opened each succeeding advance to discussion and debate. Temporarily restricted at the international level, the debate went on between the services in Washington, between the planners in the theater, and between the theater and Washington. The superabundance of advice and opinions on the value and necessity of the next operation demanded compromise and conciliation, especially when theater planners and commanders disagreed with their own service chiefs in Washington.

At SEXTANT the Allied political and military leaders had approved the general plan for an advance to the Formosa-China-Luzon area and a schedule of planned operations for 1944. While the Central Pacific forces were proceeding via the Marshalls and Carolines to the Marianas, the SWPA forces would take the Vogelkop Peninsula in New Guinea and complete the conquest of the Bismarcks by seizing Kavieng on New Ireland and Manus Island in the Admiralties. It was a schedule for planning purposes only and contained no hard and fast decisions to carry out.

With Central Pacific units in control of the Gilberts and preparing for the campaign against the Marshalls, the question of their point of assault was raised. A swing south to the Carolines would support SWPA and SOPAC forces fighting in New Guinea, on New Britain, and on Bougainville. If forces moved north against the Marianas, Truk might be bypassed, and the B-29 offensive might get under way sooner. It was possible that such a move might eventually make Formosa a more attractive target than the Philippines and lessen the importance of SWPA operations.

In January Admiral Nimitz submitted a plan to Washington covering the Central Pacific advance through 1944. He recommended an orthodox approach via the Marshalls, Carolines, Marianas, and an eventual junction with SWPA forces in the Philippines. It agreed with General MacArthur's concept that reoccupation of the Philippines would be necessary to defeat Japan.

Priority of the Central Pacific over the other Pacific routes was especially important at that point, since the imbalance of shipping and landing craft was still acute and was likely to remain so until after OVERLORD. Generals Marshall and Handy returned to Washington after a post-SEXTANT visit to the Pacific. They were aware of the SWPA's problems, and they supported General MacArthur's position that the JCS should control allocations of shipping and landing craft. They also resisted an effort to put the Kavieng operation under Admiral Nimitz instead of General MacArthur. They did agree with the Navy that theater commanders should meet and coordinate their concepts of Pacific strategy before the JCS decided what allocations should be furnished by Admiral Nimitz for completion of the conquest of the Bismarck Archipelago.

The theater conference was held at Pearl Harbor on Jan. 27–28 and attended by SWPA, SOPAC, and CPA representatives. The Army and Navy conferees agreed that greater emphasis should be placed on naval and amphibious operations along the New Guinea axis to the Philippines, rather than across the Central Pacific. The Philippines were considered a principal strategic objective. They indicated the Marianas were not important or necessary to the advance against Japan and were too far from the Japanese mainland for effective B-29 strikes. Admiral Nimitz and General MacArthur's Chief of Staff agreed that the Japanese homeland would have to be attacked from bases in China.

Although the conferees reached no decisions, General MacArthur urged the War Department that in accordance with the general opinion at the conference, all forces be concentrated—after the Marshalls operations—along the New Guinea route, the shortest and most direct path to the Philippines. All B-29s should be made available to the SWPA, rather than being based in the Marianas. Further, he desired to place all naval forces under Admiral William F. Halsey as his Allied naval commander and would welcome any British naval task forces. He concluded that since time was short and a decision essential, he was sending Major General Richard K. Sutherland to Washington to present his views.

Neither the Joint Staff planners nor Admiral King was happy with the outcome of the conference. The Admiral pointed out that the United States was committed to a two-axis advance at SEXTANT and that General MacArthur had not submitted any plan to carry out the SEXTANT decisions. The Admiral believed in the current flexible strategy and compared the success of the Central Pacific drive in the Gilberts and Marshalls with the slow progress in the SWPA. Moreover, he did not agree to putting most of the Pacific Fleet units under General MacArthur to support a New Guinea advance. He maintained also that the economical employment of the Navy required that strategic control of the Pacific remain the responsibility of a single naval commander.

In reply to Admiral King's protests General Marshall pointed out that the United States had a tremendous potential force in the Pacific provided it conformed to the basic principle of mass. Since the JCS had not reached agreement as to the route to be used to reach the Luzon and China coasts, the matter should be turned over to the JSSC for a report on the geographical objectives to be seized, the sequence in which they should be taken, and the best and quickest route or routes to be used to conclude the Pacific war. The JSSC was to assume that reinforcements would not become available until after Dec. 31, 1944. Admiral King agreed that the JSSC should handle the problem.

In the meantime the joint planners had concluded that setting up the Philippines as an essential objective was too restrictive, since the Islands might be bypassed eventually. Furthermore, they did not agree with General Sutherland that the United States should accept Mindanao as of primary importance in the Philippines. They were of the opinion that U.S. forces should stay away from the coast of China, that both axes of advance to Luzon should be used, and that the capture of the Marianas and the Palaus would be desirable.

While this difference between the theater and headquarters staffs was being debated, Admiral Nimitz sent his chief of staff, Rear Admiral Forrest P. Sherman, to Washington to present his views to the JCS. Admiral Nimitz believed that if the capture of the island of Eniwetok in the western Marshalls could be managed immediately, time schedules could be advanced, and Central Pacific forces could prepare to go into either the Carolines or the Marianas in June, since SWPA units would not be in position by that time to allow the seizure of the Palaus. A decision could be left until later on whether to go north or south of Truk, and the concept of flexibility would be preserved.

During the ensuing discussions, the Army Air Forces recommended the use of the Marianas as a B-29 base—much to General Sutherland's annoyance. To clinch the issue, the JSSC proposed that the Central Pacific route should be made the primary effort; that operations should be conducted in the Marianas and Palaus; and that the drive should continue on to Formosa or Luzon. Operations in other areas should be decided on the basis of their support of the Central Pacific offensive. General Marshall reserved judgment until he could talk with Admiral Nimitz early in March. In the meantime he felt that the JCS should continue their direction of strategy on a flexible basis, using the fleet and air arm to best advantage, and that the joint planners should study the allotment of resources, the use of land-based air superiority, and the sequence of operations in the Pacific.

As the discussions in Washington were going on, certain operations were conducted in the Pacific that affected the debate. On Feb. 15 South Pacific forces landed in the northern Solomons, a little over 100 miles from Rabaul. Truk was heavily attacked by carriers, causing the Japanese fleet to desert the base for Singapore and the Western Pacific. On Feb. 17 Central Pacific forces invaded Eniwetok, and it seemed possible that Admiral Nimitz might go into the Carolines or Marianas in June. Not to be outdone, the SWPA conducted a reconnaissance in force of the Admiralties on Feb. 29 and several days later committed a division to capture the island group. On March 5 General MacArthur announced that he would aim at Hollandia rather than Hansa Bay in mid-April.

The debate was now resolved into deciding whether Truk should be bypassed to the north with the Marianas the objective, or to the south by taking the Palaus. On March 8 General Sutherland submitted a plan that he contended would put Allied forces in the Philippines in 1944 when the Central Pacific forces would still be fighting in the Japanese mandates. But by that time Admiral Nimitz supported the Marianas undertaking, which was also endorsed by the JSSC. One of General Sutherland's arguments against the Marianas was that they could not serve as a base to mount major operations against the China-Formosa-Luzon area because of their restricted facilities. Admiral King countered by pointing out that division assaults could be mounted in other areas and rendezvous at sea as they had for TORCH. He added that few localities along the New Guinea coast were suitable for staging areas and that it would soon become a rear area of little importance.

On March 12 the JCS issued a directive that was a compromise agreement. Hollandia was approved for April 15. Truk was to be bypassed to the north, and the Marianas were to be invaded on June 15. In September the forces would move southward, at which time the Palaus would be seized by Central Pacific troops in preparation for the big move by SWPA forces into Mindanao on Nov. 15. Undecided was whether Formosa or Luzon would be the next objective, but a target of Feb. 15 was established. The SWPA was given the responsibility for planning for Luzon and the POA for Formosa. All Marine units, naval support, and combat loaders were to be returned by General MacArthur by May 5; however, when the target date for Hollandia was changed to April 22, the JCS granted the SWPA a week's extension for the retention of POA forces and equipment.

On the surface that appeared to be a setback for General MacArthur, as he had been turned down on his plan for concentration on the New Guinea axis, bypassing Truk to the south, and taking Havieng. His greatest ambition was still on the agenda: He was still slated to lead the Allied forces back to the Philippines.

Although the swiftly changing pattern of Pacific strategy was deceptive, the JCS retained the two-axis advance by the SWPA and the Central Pacific, and the same general objective, the Formosa-Luzon-China coast area. The Pacific strategy was settled insofar as the concept of flexibility would permit. Now the JCS and the Joint Staff planners were confronted with another urgent problem that had been awaiting the strategic decisions; namely, the breakup of the South Pacific area and the reallocation of its forces.

The Dissolution of SOPAC Forces

As far back as October 1943, Lieutenant General Millard F. Harmon, commander of the South Pacific Army, realized that the role of his Army command would be coming to an end in the spring of 1944. Established in July 1942 to maintain a strategic defensive, the

Guadalcanal campaign and the succeeding drive through the Solomons had changed its mission to one of active participation in an offensive aimed at the capture of Rabaul. The Army troops in General Harmon's command were under the direct operational control of Admiral Halsey, who, in turn, received general strategic direction from General MacArthur. The complicated chain of command resulted from the entry of South Pacific forces by early 1943 into territory that had been formally placed under General MacArthur. As soon as Rabaul was isolated and the Allies controlled the Bismarcks, South Pacific forces would be available.

The Army and Navy planners were undecided whether the reallocation of forces should precede or follow the determination of strategy, although there was little question as to how they wished to assign them. There was little if any argument over the ground forces, naval forces, and assault craft. The discussion concerned the assignment of the Thirteenth Air Force and the timing of the transfer of South Pacific troops and equipment. It was the Navy's contention that the redeployment of the troops should await the conclusion of the then-scheduled Kavieng-Manus operations, since Admiral Halsey depended on the Thirteenth Air Force for support. Both General Marshall and General Arnold, however, wished to keep this air force intact and preferred to give General MacArthur immediate operational command so that he could employ it most advantageously and coordinate the air effort with the SWPA's Fifth Air Force. Later on, General MacArthur was given complete control of the Thirteenth Air Force.

In mid-March the Joint Chiefs accepted the recommendations of the joint planners, which resulted in a division of South Pacific resources and forces more or less on service lines. After the Hollandia operation in April, General MacArthur would receive one corps and six divisions and control of the Thirteenth Air Force. He was also assured that all combat and service troops not required in the South Pacific would eventually be sent to his area. Considering the shortages of service troops, that was an important matter. Except for specific units assigned to the Seventh Fleet in the SWPA, the bulk of naval resources was to be given to Admiral Nimitz, along with all naval and Marine air units, the two Marine divisions, and the Marine Amphibious Corps. General MacArthur would assist Admiral Nimitz in providing long-range bombardment of Truk and the Palaus, and the details of the transfers were to be arranged by the two commanders.

During March the Army planners began to study the problem of

Army command reorganization in the Central Pacific and the future assignment of General Harmon and his staff. They recommended that there should be an overall Army commander in the POA and also an overall Army Air commander who would be responsible for Twentieth Air Force units situated in Pacific Ocean areas. The Hawaiian Department and South Pacific area should be established as communications areas. In May General Marshall approved the recommendations and informed Lieutenant General Robert C. Richardson, Jr., that he would become Commanding General, U.S. Army Forces in Pacific Ocean Areas, and that Harmon would be the new overall Air commander as well as Deputy Commander, Twentieth Air Force. General Harmon was made directly responsible to Admiral Nimitz for all operational matters and placed under General Richardson for such administrative control as was necessary. The new command arrangement was to become effective on Aug. 1.

The prospective changeover on Aug. 1 from an active theater of operations into a staging and rehabilitation area indicated the forward progress of the war. The two-axis drive that had marked the beginning of the Allied offensive in the Pacific in 1942 had become one, and a new thrust was advancing in the Central Pacific. Some of the South Pacific resources would go to the SWPA, some to the Central Pacific, and the remainder would support both areas. The division served to strengthen the concept that the Pacific would continue to be fought on two fronts: the fundamentally Army approach of the SWPA and the essentially naval advance of the POA. The consistent inability of the Army and the Navy to agree on an overall commander for the Pacific would also tend to support the maintenance of the double offensive rather than the consolidation of forces and employment of the principle of mass and concentration so typical of the U.S. position in the European war.

The reallocation of South Pacific resources did not meet the requirements of the SWPA and POA, and deficiencies soon appeared to complicate the planning for further advances in the Pacific. Certainly, strategy could be worked out and combat forces assigned to implement the strategic concept, but without transportation and logistical support the other two would be powerless.

Service Troops and Transportation

Early in 1944 the need for service troops in the Pacific was more acute than ever. Worldwide shortages of that manpower group were inevitably magnified by OVERLORD. General Marshall had urged all theater commanders in January to roll up their nonessential rear bases and employ the minimum number of service troops in intermediate areas. Savings might be made by concentrating supply and administrative functions and moving headquarters units forward quickly. Whenever feasible, civilians should be employed to reduce service troop requirements.

General MacArthur protested that any reductions in service troops in the field would slow the tempo of operations and permit the Japanese to consolidate their positions. "The great problem of warfare in the Pacific is to move forces into contact and maintain them. Victory is dependent upon the solution of the logistic problem." He considered his requirements for service troops so essential that he recommended that uncommitted combat units in the United States should be converted for that purpose if necessary.

Other Allied countries were feeling the manpower shortages in early 1944. New Zealand and Australia both requested advice from the CCS on ways and means to reduce their armed forces to meet potential manpower shortages in food production areas. In March the CCS informed New Zealand that its 3d Division in Italy would be sent home when conditions permitted and that two New Zealand brigade groups would be withdrawn from the Solomons after the projected end of the Bismarck campaign in May. The CCS approved also an Australian proposal to reduce its overall military forces to six full-strength and combat-ready divisions by the end of 1944. That would result in demobilizing some 30,000 Australians during the remainder of 1944. Although those additions to the home forces would assist New Zealand and Australia to support themselves, they would not solve the U.S. service troop problem, since both areas were rapidly becoming rear zones remote from the combat area.

In the meantime, however, other factors were adversely affecting the American service troop predicament. There was a steady flow of divisions and supporting units from the United States and Hawaii in the first half of 1944. In November 1943 the SWPA had only four U.S. Army divisions. Additional divisions, arriving from the Central Pacific, Hawaii, and the United States, brought the total to eight divisions by June 1944. In November 1943 four U.S. Army divisions were also in the South Pacific, augmented in January 1944 by one division from Hawaii and one from the United States. The transfer of those six Army divisions to SWPA control by July 1944 would provide General MacArthur with fourteen Army divisions. The transfer of the three divisions from Hawaii left the Central Pacific with only two Army divisions in November 1943, but by June 1944 four additional divisions had arrived from the United

States. Thus, a total of twenty U.S. Army divisions was in the Pacific in June 1944 as compared to thirteen during the SEXTANT Conference.

The increase in the number of divisions, with their supporting units and their movement into forward areas, entailed longer lines of communications, more construction to be completed, more bases to be manned, and more ships to transport the men and equipment to perform those tasks. Although some service troops could be acquired by shutting down old bases and facilities in the rear areas, labor problems in the forward areas would mount, and local help would be at a minimum until the Philippines were reached. It therefore appeared that the service troop shortages would continue to prevail at least until 1945.

The buildup of the divisions and their supporting troops magnified another problem: the availability of cargo and personnel shipping to maintain the forces and to enable them to participate in the offensive against Japan. The Army planners expected the troop-shipping backlog to be made up by June 1944, but that a dry cargo ship deficiency would develop at about that time. Assault landing craft and transports would not be available for the Pacific until after the OVERLORD assault.

To conserve shipping, a new system was put into effect in transferring divisions between the United States, Hawaii, and the South–Southwest Pacific. The same transports that unloaded a division in Hawaii would pick up another division there and convey it to the SWPA. The equipment and supplies of the division off-loaded in Hawaii would remain loaded and transferred to the division bound for the SWPA, leaving its own for the division debarking in Hawaii. Such procedure not only coordinated the troop transfers, but saved considerable time by eliminating off-loading and on-loading of divisional equipment. It also took some of the strain off the port facilities in Hawaii.

Despite those economies, it was evident that a cargo ship shortage would develop around May; so, in March, General MacArthur was asked if he could release any of the seventy-six Liberty ships operating in the SWPA. His reply indicated that not only would he have to keep what he had, but he would require sizable additions to his cargo fleet during the summer if he were to carry out the instructions of the JCS. When Admiral Nimitz also requested ship increases, the JCS decided to approve the requirements of both commanders for April and to call a shipping conference in Washington to survey the overall situation. In advising the SWPA and POA of the conference, the JCS expressed its concern: "The shortage in shipping during the coming months may affect the strategy of the war in both Europe and the Pacific, unless all concerned exercise the most rigid economy and adopt all possible expedients to conserve both personnel and cargo shipping."

The serious situation was saved by General Eisenhower's decisions. In March ANVIL was canceled as a simultaneous attack to coincide with OVERLORD, and in April it was postponed indefinitely; and the landing craft and shipping earmarked for ANVIL were reallocated. The reallocation enabled the JCS to meet the shipping requirements of General MacArthur and Admiral Nimitz through July 1944, but the assault- and landing-craft shortages continued to be acute. Transfers were made of those resources between the POA and SWPA, which helped to ease the shortages. In the Pacific, however, no real solution to the assault- and landing-craft shortage could be anticipated until after the Normandy invasion.

Now, however, both General MacArthur and Admiral Nimitz would be able to proceed with their planned operations for the summer of 1944, and in the meantime new developments conceivably could enable or make unnecessary further increments of shipping and landing craft. By June at least the shipping situation had improved, but the service troop situation was far from satisfactory and gave few indications of early improvement.

The Pacific War Status in June 1944

The war against Japan had made considerable progress by the eve of OVERLORD. General MacArthur's forces had advanced along the northern coast of New Guinea as far as Biak Island. The Admiralties were firmly held by the Allies, and large groups of Japanese had been bypassed in the Bismarcks. Central Pacific forces were on the verge of advancing from the Marshalls into the Marianas to begin isolating Truk and the Carolines. Only in CBI was the picture less rosy, but even there favorable indications were appearing. General Stilwell was on the offensive at Myitkyina, and Lord Mountbatten had stopped the Japanese near Imphal. But in eastern China the new Japanese drive had assumed serious proportions that seemed. likely to have serious consequences in China.

Several important strategic changes occurred in the six-month period following SEXTANT. Foremost among them was the decline of CBI in strategic importance. Pacific strategy had changed in details but it remained essentially the same. The main objectives remained constant; only the intermediate had been altered in conformity with a new set of circumstances. It had been agreed that flexibility would be the accepted policy and that General MacArthur and Admiral Nimitz would maintain their separate domains for the time being.

In the conduct of the war, improvements in the Allied technique of amphibious warfare had enabled the acceleration of the SWPA and POA campaigns to continue. Increasing airpower and naval power had forced the Japanese fleet to withdraw to safer waters. In the CBI theater, air transport aircraft had emerged as a powerful weapon to aid jungle warfare troops, and the B-29's were preparing to demonstrate their long-range offensive capabilities.

In the war ahead with Japan the logistical difficulties were serious obstacles that threatened to slow the momentum. The urgent need to resolve the service troop shortages and the constant danger of shipping- and landing-craft deficits could prove more difficult to work out than the strategic and tactical problems. Until those obstacles could be overcome, the progress of the war and the selection of objectives might very well depend upon logistics instead of strategy.

No far-reaching relief could be expected until after OVERLORD, and until the end of the war in Europe was in sight. Then a final solution of the logistics and strategy problems could be reached. Unexpected and competing demands had come up for U.S. manpower, aircraft, landing craft, and shipping. To provide an adequate OVERLORD assault force and still satisfy the demands of the British in the Mediterranean, General MacArthur and Admiral Nimitz in the Pacific, and Generalissimo Chiang Kai-shek in China, critical adjustments had been made and calculated risks taken in the wars against Germany and Japan. By early June everything depended on the outcome of OVERLORD. For the strategic planners in Washington, London, and Algiers, the past, present, and future were converged on Operation OVERLORD. After three years of planning, General Marshall and his staff could only sit back and wait.

In the predawn hours of June 5, General Eisenhower made his historic decision to proceed with the invasion despite weather forecasts of choppy seas and unfavorable winds. On June 6 the ships and craft of the mightiest armada ever assembled headed through the rough waters of the Channel toward the beaches of Normandy. With them went the hopes and prayers of the free world.

Chapter VI

The London Conference

On June 6, 1944, the successful landings of Allied troops in Normandy ended an anxious waiting period for General Marshall and the War Department staff. The operation symbolized the consummation of a strategic concept, to strike at the heart of Germany, which had finally been agreed upon by the Allies at Tehran. The success of OVERLORD was a triumph for the American principles of mass concentration and of waging a decisive war. With the capture of Rome on June 4, the Allied offensive picture in Europe changed almost overnight. The long months of frustration in Italy and the equally long months of waiting in the United Kingdom had ended. The time for decision on the future course of the Mediterranean war had arrived.

As Allied armies pushed forward into northern Italy, the debate was renewed between the British proponents for continuing the Italian campaign and the American supporters of Operation ANVIL. Would the prize be the occupation of all Italy, the capture of Istria and the Ljubljana Gap with all the associated political and strategic consequences for the Balkans, or the direct support of OVERLORD and the occupation of southern France? In other words, was the conclusion of the European conflict to be a matter of political or military strategy? The Americans and the British were each confident that their concept would assist OVERLORD by either pinning down or drawing off German troops that might otherwise oppose General Eisenhower's forces. The moment of truth had arrived. The Allies would have to continue a strong, active offensive in the Mediterranean or throw their forces into the assault on Germany from the west and be satisfied with a holding role in Italy.

U.S. ARMY PHOTOGRAPH

Allied invasion chiefs at a press conference in Allied Command Headquarters, London. Left to right: Lt. Gen. Omar N. Bradley, Commander, U.S. Army Ground Forces; Adm. Sir Bertram H. Ramsay, Allied Naval Commander; Air Chief Marshal Sir Arthur Tedder, Deputy Supreme Commander; Gen Dwight D. Eisenhower, Supreme Commander; Gen. Sir Bernard Montgomery, Commander in Chief, British Armies; Air Chief Marshall Sir Trafford Leigh-Mallory; and Lt. Gen. Walter Bedell-Smith, Chief of Staff.

The ANVIL Debates

The U.S. Chiefs of Staff flew to England for an informal conference with the British shortly after OVERLORD was launched. The U.S. Chiefs wanted to be on hand should either of two contingencies arise: the Allied forces had gained only an insecure footing in the beachhead area, and the CCS might be forced to decide whether to withdraw or continue the operation; a German counterattack might be mounted seven or eight days after D Day, and might require CCS action. Since the visit was of a precautionary nature, the JCS advised the British that they would be accompanied by a small planning staff and would not be prepared for a full-dress conference. Unless a crisis in OVERLORD occurred, the meetings would be informal and the discussions general.

The CCS met for discussions on June 10, 11, 13, 14, and 15; they visited the Normandy beachhead on June 12. The German counterattack, which had been expected, failed to develop because Hitler and some of his staff were convinced that the Allied forces remaining in the United Kingdom were going to make another landing, probably along the Channel coast. Thus, while strong German troops were held in the Channel area, the Allies were reinforcing their positions in Normandy.

With the Allies in Normandy seemingly secure, the CCS were able to consider Mediterranean, Pacific, and Far Eastern matters as well as the invasion of northwest Europe. It was generally agreed that an amphibious operation should be conducted from the Mediterranean during midsummer, but, confronted with a fluid situation in both France and Italy, the CCS decided to hold the options open as to time and place.

General Marshall pointed out that fifteen additional combat landing craft were to be made available for the Mediterranean operation, and he evinced an interest in the possibilities of a landing at Sète on the Gulf of Lions. That operation could possibly be exploited through the Carcassonne Gap and conceivably could open up a port on the Bay of Biscay through which more troops could be landed to assist OVERLORD. He was especially concerned with moving American divisions out of the United States into action on the main front as rapidly as possible. Now that OVERLORD seemed to be going well, the Allies could take more time to make a decision; but he thought that the target date for any Mediterranean operation should be July 25.

If the operations were to be against southern France, Field Marshall Sir Alan Brooke, Admiral King, and Admiral Sir Andrew B.

Cunningham were inclined to agree with General Marshall that the landings should be at Sète. Little consideration was given to an assault in the Marseille-Toulon-Riviera area similar to those envisaged by the joint planners for ANVIL. If the Soviets launched an offensive toward the Balkans, Admiral King and Air Chief Marshal Sir Charles Portal believed that an Anglo-American drive might be launched against the Istrian Peninsula. A third alternative might be a direct descent by sea on the Bay of Biscay, provided the OVERLORD forces had reached the Loire River.

With those three possibilities in mind, as well as the original ANVIL operation, the CCS instructed Generals Eisenhower and Wilson that the latter would be responsible for planning for ANVIL, the Sète operation, and the Istrian venture, whereas General Eisenhower would plan for the Bay of Biscay. The operation decided upon would be conducted on a three-division lift basis. The two generals would arrange between themselves the release of landing craft for the operation and troop carrier aircraft for a supporting paratroop operation. A final decision on the four options would be made on the basis of the progress of OVERLORD and the Soviet offensive, but the July 25 target date was to be achieved if possible. So, provided the Pisa-Rimini line in Italy was reached by late July, an ANVIL type of operation was back on the books.

Back in Washington the JWPC had studied the four choices and concluded with a strong recommendation for ANVIL. They contended that ANVIL would open up more ports quickly, help OVERLORD directly by drawing off or pinning down more German troops, and make the most effective use of French troops. The Army planners agreed with the JWPC estimate if OVERLORD went according to schedule; but if it should be stopped, then an operation via Sète, Toulouse, and Bordeaux, or the direct seizure of St. Nazaire and Nantes and a subsequent move against Bordeaux might be in order. The Strategy Section doubted that General Wilson had sufficient forces to undertake operations against Istria, followed by an advance through northern Italy toward Ljubljana Gap. Further, winter weather and the poor line of communications would make it difficult to support, the French would be likely to protest the use of their troops in the Balkans, and little relief of pressure on OVERLORD would result. The Strategy Section did not overlook the possible political consequences of invading the Balkans, and took into account the risk of becoming involved in civil wars in Greece and Yugoslavia. One member of the Section observed, "Had we adopted a strategy

U.S. ARMY PHOTOGRAPH

General Dwight D. Eisenhower (center), accompanied by General George C. Marshall (left) and Admiral Ernest J. King stand in an amphibious "DUCK" as they tour Vierville sur Mer, northern France, June 12, 1944.

to defeat Germany politically and economically, then the suggested operation might be considered."

While the various Mediterranean courses of action were being debated, General Marshall had flown from England to Italy to confer with General Wilson and his commanders. General Marshall was successful in convincing General Wilson of the urgent Allied requirement for a major port through which forty to fifty divisions in the United States could be sent to OVERLORD. On June 19 General Wilson approved the ANVIL operation with an Aug. 15 target date provided the CCS agreed that the need for a port was paramount. Otherwise, he would prefer to advance in Italy toward Ljubljana Gap and southern Hungary.

Neither General Marshall nor General Eisenhower favored an Adriatic diversion, and both urged that ANVIL be launched as soon as practicable. General Marshall commented: "There should be no delay in getting a firm decision on ANVIL if we are to provide the necessary additional resources in time to make it possible to launch the operation at an earlier date than August 15th." General Eisenhower pointed out the need for large ports, and he was sure that the capture of Marseille would furnish a more direct route northward for Allied forces to join in the battle for the Ruhr. He was willing to provide the additional resources only for ANVIL because he was convinced that the Allies could support only one major theater in the European war—and that was the OVERLORD battle area. He was solidly backed by President Roosevelt and the JCS. The SHAEF staff did not like the Bay of Biscay operation, and they discarded the Sète undertaking because of the timing. So the Americans were again pushing for ANVIL.

In the meantime the British had decided to support operations into northern Italy and the Ljubljana Gap as the most useful employment for General Wilson's forces. With Generals Wilson and Alexander arguing for a continuation of the current offensive, the Prime Minister and the British Chiefs strove valiantly to save the Italian campaigns. Churchill aimed his efforts at the President and General Eisenhower, while the British Chiefs endeavored to persuade their U.S. opposite numbers. The British did not accept the need for another major port because there were enough small ports in Normandy that could be adequately enlarged. Nor did they view ANVIL as the operation most helpful to OVERLORD. They were, however, willing to release to OVERLORD at a later date some of the divisions designated for ANVIL, but they believed that the pressure against the Germans in Italy should be maintained. General

Eisenhower should retain his landing craft to exploit the use of any small ports he might capture. Meanwhile, Generals Wilson and Alexander would present a threat to southern France as they advanced into northern Italy.

The Americans did not withdraw from their position. The U.S. Joint Chiefs informed the British Chiefs that the JCS could not accept Italy as a decisive theater, and that the delay now taking place in reaching agreement on ANVIL was not consistent with the early termination of the war. Further, the President felt that General Eisenhower's judgment in the matter should be respected. He also informed Churchill that General Wilson had already enough forces to carry on the drive in Italy.

In an attempt to persuade the President, the Prime Minister made an intensive appeal on behalf of operations in the Italian theater. He emphasized the support of General Wilson, Field Marshals Alexander and Jan Christiaan Smuts for an operation eastward across the Adriatic and the capture of Trieste. Evidently he was thinking in terms of the political results of a major victory in Italy, especially for the Balkans. He argued that "Political considerations, such as the revolt of populations against the enemy or the submission and coming over of his satellites, are a valid and important factor. . . ." to hasten the end of the European war. Political strategy must be merged with military strategy. The British Chiefs pointed out that the CCS, not General Eisenhower, were responsible for deciding European strategy. They also stated that there would not be enough air resources for both Italy and ANVIL.

The President was adamant and informed Churchill: "The exploitation of 'OVERLORD,' our victorious advances in ITALY, an early assault on Southern France, combined with the Soviet drives to the west—will most surely serve to realize our object—the unconditional surrender of Germany." He also reminded Churchill that Premier Stalin had favored ANVIL, and that the Soviet leader would have to be informed of any change in plans. Regarding political objectives, the President stated, "I agree that the political considerations you mention are important factors, but military operations based thereon must be definitely secondary to the primary operations of striking at the heart of Germany." He continued that to conduct an operation against Istria would be to disregard two important considerations—the agreed grand strategy for an early defeat of Germany, and the time factor involved in a campaign to debouch from the Ljubljana Gap into Slovenia and Hungary. He doubted whether more than six divisions could be fighting beyond the Ljubljana Gap within a decisive period on purely logistical grounds.

The President declared, "I cannot agree to the employment of United States troops against Istria and into the Balkans, nor can I see the French agreeing to such use of French troops." If ANVIL were not launched, the whole question of French troops would have to be reopened. He concluded, "Finally, for purely political considerations over here, I should never survive even a slight setback in 'OVERLORD' if it were known that fairly large forces had been diverted to the Balkans."

Years later Churchill wrote, "It was his [the President's] objections to a descent on the Istrian peninsula and a thrust against Vienna through the Ljubljana Gap that revealed both the rigidity of the American military plans and his own suspicion of what he called a campaign 'in the Balkans.' " In the Prime Minister's opinion, Istria and Trieste were strategic and political positions that "might exercise profound and widespread reactions, especially after the Russian advances."

Nevertheless, on July 2 the President asked the Prime Minister to authorize a directive to General Wilson to start preparations for an early ANVIL. He declared, "I am compelled by the logic of not dispersing our main efforts to a new theater to agree with my Chiefs of Staff. . . . I always think of my early geometry—'a straight line is the shortest distance between two points.' " Rather than permit an impasse to develop, the Prime Minister consented to a directive to General Wilson. ANVIL would be launched with an Aug. 15 target date on a three-division assault basis; the amount of airborne lift to be determined later. The buildup would be to ten divisions; all other resources would be devoted to the Italian campaign. Generals Eisenhower and Wilson were to arrange between themselves the transfer of additional resources.

Preparations for ANVIL went ahead during July. In view of the worldwide shortage of service troops, those troops would have to be withdrawn from Italy. Combat loaders and landing craft were transferred from SHAEF to the Mediterranean, and by July 20 General Eisenhower had sent 416 tow planes and 225 glider pilots to the Mediterranean for the ANVIL airlift. General Jacob L. Devers was appointed to command ANVIL, and his army group would consist of the U.S. Seventh Army, commanded by Lieutenant General Alexander M. Patch, and the French forces. General Eisenhower would take over the army group as soon as sufficient progress had been made in France.

Early in August, shortly after the Allies broke through St. Lô, the British made their last attempt to cancel ANVIL, which had been renamed DRAGOON on Aug. 1. Churchill and the British Chiefs tried again to persuade the President and the U.S. Chiefs either to land the ANVIL forces through the ports in Brittany or to allow them to remain in Italy for an advance through the Ljubljana Gap. When the Americans pointed out that the condition of the ports was unknown and that they might be destroyed before capture, the British concentrated on the advantages of the campaign in Italy and eastward. Churchill endeavored to persuade General Eisenhower to change his position on DRAGOON. He also asked Harry Hopkins of the Lend-Lease Administration to intercede and influence General Marshall.

The British maneuvers were received by the Washington planners with something less than enthusiasm. Preparations for DRAGOON were well advanced and the joint planners considered any change to a Brittany landing impracticable, since southern France operations were predicated on a fast turnaround of shipping, and change would result in a delay in releasing shipping to other areas. Further, the planners felt that weather conditions and poor lines of communication would make Balkan operations very difficult.

Despite the British efforts, General Eisenhower stood firmly by his position and maintained that DRAGOON was the best concomitant for OVERLORD. He was backed by the President, the JCS, and Hopkins, and the British finally conceded defeat on Aug. 8 and endeavored to salvage what they could of the Italian campaign.

After an intensive sea and air bombardment of the coast, General Patch's Seventh Army landed in southern France between Cannes and Hyères on Aug. 15. The Allied forces consisted of 3 U.S. divisions, 7 French divisions, and 1 U.S.–British airborne division. The German High Command had considered pulling back the 11 German divisions in southern France to a defensive line closer to the German border prior to the Allied landings, but that had not been done. However, when the German staff learned that the landings were in force, they ordered their troops south of the Loire River to withdraw toward Germany. As a result the Allied divisions moved rapidly inland, encountering only scattered resistance, and by Sept. 11 they had joined up with the OVERLORD forces in northern France.

Thus, after more than two years of discussion, the Anglo-American debate over the Mediterranean and cross-Channel operations was finally ended. Despite strenuous British attempts to win another reprieve for the Mediterranean, the American insistence on strengthening the OVERLORD assault held firm and put an end to ambitious British plans for the Mediterranean.

The Allied forces remaining in Italy were strong enough to keep pressure on the German troops, but they were inadequate to strike a decisive blow that would have finished the Italian campaign and permitted a penetration of Austria and the Balkans. Until the last few weeks of the European war, the front lines in Italy remained practically static, and the Mediterranean Theater of Operations was to become, like the CBI, a holding theater. The decline of the MTO confirmed the successful strategic concept of a concentrated, decisive war against Germany.

The Asiatic Holding Theater

The Allied decision to launch ANVIL was one of the most important made during the summer of 1944—but the war against Japan was soon to become the main topic of military discussions. During the London Conference the CCS considered the future of SEAC and CBI, and the British again expressed their intention of taking a prominent part in the war against Japan. They reported that Lord Mountbatten would seek to clear the Kohima-Imphal Road, take Myitkyina, and build up a defensive area south of Mogaung-Myitkyina. The object was to assure the maximum flow of supplies to China. The Americans stated that the U.S. combat air strength in China had reached its peak. That was a natural consequence of the declining importance of CBI in U.S. strategic planning.

During the spring of 1944 the Japanese had pushed into Honan Province from the north and south to open a rail route between north and central China. Twentieth Air Force tonnage was diverted, and heavy bombers were used as transports to provide General Chennault with additional tonnage to slow the Japanese advance. General Arnold suggested that General Chennault should either receive at least 8,000 tons a month for the Fourteenth Air Force, or the United States should pull everything out because General Chennault could not accomplish his mission on less tonnage. The proposal was turned down by the Army planners because 8,000 tons could not be allocated and, for political reasons, China could not be deserted. Requests from the Generalissimo and General Chennault to use B-29 stocks in China and to employ B-29 bombers on tactical missions against Japanese targets in eastern China were disapproved by the JCS during June.

Confronted with the prospect of a defeat for the Chinese, General Marshall asked General Stilwell on July 1 if he (Stilwell) could do anything to improve the China situation. General Stilwell replied affirmatively—if he were placed in command of the Chinese forces. General Marshall obtained JCS and Presidential approval to promote Stilwell to a full general and to urge Generalissimo Chiang Kai-shek to accept him as overall commander. The Generalissimo agreed in principle to the President's proposal, but weeks went by without further developments. When subsequent requests brought no response, the President sent Major General Patrick J. Hurley as his personal representative to Chungking in August.

In July the Japanese had supplemented their southern drive by launching another attack north from Canton. It was apparent that the Japanese would eventually threaten and perhaps neutralize U.S. airfields in eastern China. If that were accomplished, the Fourteenth Air Force would be unable to provide much support for the Pacific advance. Hump tonnage in June was more than 18,000 tons and by the end of summer would amount to almost 30,000 tons a month. The increase, however, did not relieve the situation in eastern China as much as had been expected, since the problem of internal distribution within China still remained critical, and large stores piled up at the forward termini of the Hump run, far behind the front area. Although General Chennault was given first priority on Hump tonnage, he was unable to halt the Japanese advance, and by the time of the second Quebec (OCTAGON) conference in mid-September, the Japanese were closing in on Kweilin.

Meanwhile, in early September, General Hurley arrived in Chungking and secured the Generalissimo's approval of General Stilwell as overall commander. But negotiations to effect General Stilwell's assumption of command dragged on for another month and finally ended in a disagreement between the General and Chiang Kai-shek. General Stilwell was recalled from China in October.

While the situation in China was deteriorating, the Allied attack in Burma was progressing. The Japanese fell back from the Imphal region during July, and General Stilwell's forces succeeded in destroying the enemy resistance at Myitkyina in August. Despite those developments, the military objectives in Burma were indefinite. On June 3 the CCS directive to Lord Mountbatten had instructed him to concentrate on building up the air route to China, meanwhile pressing "advantages against the enemy." Such vague terminology was not very informative; nevertheless SEAC headquarters developed two plans that were presented to the CCS for consideration. One plan envisaged the capture of Mandalay by the familiar three-pronged assault, with British troops operating from the west and the Ledo and Yunnan Chinese approaching from the north and east. A second plan projected an airborne and seaborne assault on Rangoon. Lord Mountbatten went to London in early August to present the two plans.

The United States favored the Mandalay plan, since it would extend the protection of the air route farther south and keep the forces currently occupied in northern Burma usefully employed. U.S. intelligence sources did not believe any operations in Burma would influence enemy dispositions in the Pacific, but the joint planners felt that the Mandalay plan was more in phase with the U.S. timing of Pacific operations. The British favored the Rangoon operations as the best means to end the Burma commitment, but it depended on the end of the war in Europe for forces and resources. In mid-August the JCS turned down a British request to delay SEAC operations in northern Burma until forces to take Rangoon became available. The JCS urged acceptance of the Mandalay plan, with the Rangoon operation to be undertaken in 1945 if all went well. No decision had been made when the second Quebec conference convened in September.

During the summer of 1944, with SEAC strategy undecided, the War Department planners studied the role of the United States in future operations in CBI. In August General Marshall stated that no U.S. divisions were scheduled for CBI in 1945, and the following month he turned down the Prime Minister's request for U.S. divisions to bolster the Burma offensive, observing that all divisions were allocated to the European or Pacific theaters. The Army had never been inclined to involve large bodies of U.S. ground forces in Burma and China, but now a sentiment was growing in the War Department favoring a gradual withdrawal of all U.S. forces in Burma.

The Strategy Section, OPD, recommended that since the main objective of U.S. forces was to assist China, U.S. and Chinese forces should be withdrawn from Burma after Lashio was reached so that the British could reconquer their own colonial empire and the United States would not receive the stigma of helping them resubjugate the native populace. That sort of political awareness was typical of Army strategic planning during the summer of 1944 when the problems of peace began to weigh more heavily on the military staff. Although the United States was committed to aid China, it was now a limited commitment merely to keep China in the war. The U.S. acceptance of CBI as a holding theater, in which the enemy could be kept occupied while the decisive engagements of the war were being fought in the Pacific, was now complete.

Objective—The Philippines

During the London conference the CCS also considered various courses of action that might be followed to defeat the Japanese. Prior to leaving Washington for the conference, the JCS decided to re-examine all plans for operations after the Marianas to determine whether the war tempo in the Pacific could be accelerated. The CCS discussed proposals to bypass the Philippines and Palaus to surprise the Japanese at Formosa and an alternative possibility of bypassing Formosa and going directly to Kyushu. The general agreement was that it was important to do the unexpected when fighting the Japanese, but they found it difficult to decide just what form the unexpected should take. The Americans then decided to query their Pacific commanders.

The reduction of Japanese air effectiveness, the prospects of successful, decisive fleet engagements that would permit U.S. forces greater freedom of action, the indication that the enemy was strengthening his Philippines–northern NEI defenses, and the recent enemy drive in China that might preclude or decrease the air support of Pacific operations, confirmed the impression of the War Department staff that a reassessment of objectives was in order.

At the same time the Allied desire to remain flexible in Pacific strategy and yet do the unexpected had to be reconciled with strong influences that were inclined to shape Pacific strategy along definite lines. General MacArthur was the most important of those. He responded to the JCS query from London swiftly and negatively. His target dates could not be advanced because of logistical considerations. The suggestion of bypassing the Philippines and advancing toward either Formosa or the Japanese mainland was utterly unsound. The Philippines were necessary in a strategic sense, and also the United States had a moral obligation to liberate the Filipinos.

Although the joint planners agreed that it would not be feasible to accelerate the Pacific campaign, they did not see the military necessity for capturing Mindanao. They considered the Palaus essential for any further advance, either into the Philippines or to points north. With Japanese strength increasing in the Philippines, they felt that bypassing them should be considered.

By late June the war in the Pacific was described by Admiral King as being in a "crossing in the ocean" phase, during which most of the fighting consisted of amphibious assaults to seize small islands or limited beachheads. POA forces were struggling bitterly for Saipan in the Marianas and SWPA troops were leapfrogging up the northern coast of New Guinea.

The joint planners laid out two courses that would be open to the United States until the Mindanao operations scheduled for November 1944 were begun: the first lay through the Philippines, Formosa, and Ryukyus to Kyushu and Honshu, and the other via the Bonins to either Kyushu or Hokkaido and then to Honshu. The first involved the control or capture of large land masses, but was a steady and sure route. The second was quicker but more dangerous, depending upon the ability of the Navy and its carrier planes to control the air and sea.

While the Washington planners were outlining bold, opportunistic courses of action, the Pacific theater commanders became more cautious. In early July Admiral Nimitz favored the strategy already agreed upon and indicated it might be difficult to meet the established target dates. He thought that General MacArthur's basic concept of advancing land-based air forces, ground troops, and naval forces at the same time was sound.

A theater staff conference was held at Pearl Harbor in early July to consider speeding up operations. POA and SWPA agreed that the scheduled operations should be retained. Admiral Nimitz again supported General MacArthur's concept of moving forward en masse, but he did not agree to the necessity of taking Luzon before Formosa. A setback to the Japanese Fleet might permit the Americans to bypass Luzon. However, no decision between Luzon and Formosa needed to be made immediately.

The Pearl Harbor conference of July 27–28 between the President, General MacArthur, and Admiral Nimitz failed to clarify the Pacific strategy. General MacArthur presented his brief for the Philippines, and Admiral Nimitz gave his for Formosa, although he agreed that a need for Luzon might develop. Despite the lack of decisions at the conference, it helped the President to familiarize himself with Pacific problems and brought agreement between the two commanders on fundamental strategy. Oddly enough, neither of them raised the issue of service troop shortages.

At a conference on Aug. 7 at SWPA headquarters, attended by a number of officers from the War Department, General MacArthur announced that he could conduct the Luzon campaign within six weeks at a maximum and probably in less than thirty days. As for Formosa, he doubted the ability of SWPA air to neutralize Japanese bases in Luzon before an operation against Formosa could be mounted. Moreover, logistics and service troop shortages made the operation against Formosa impracticable.

During the early summer, pressure from the Navy had been in-

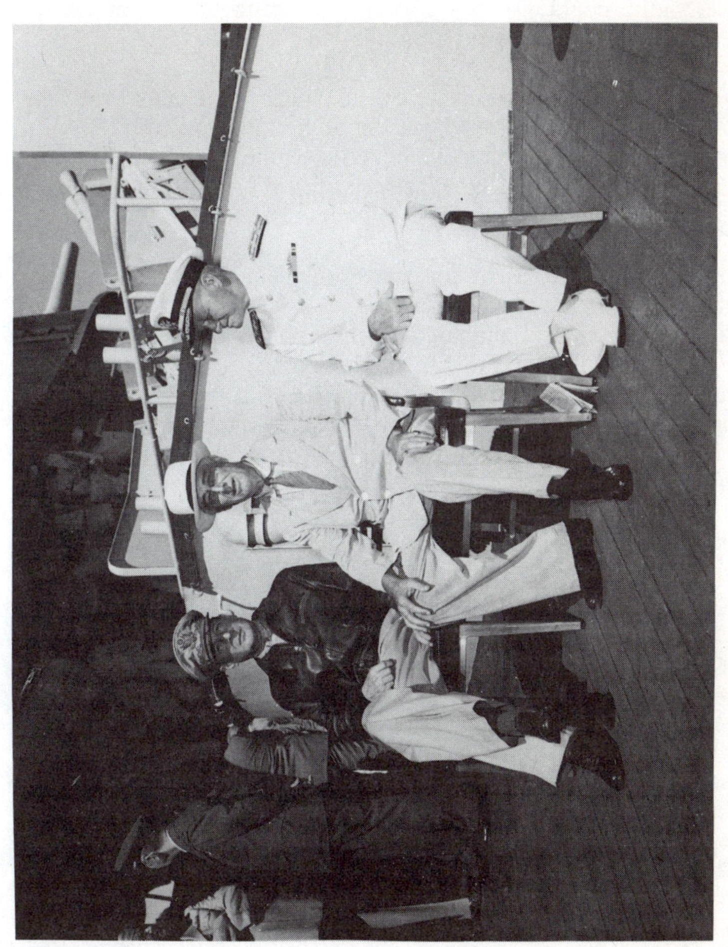

U.S. ARMY PHOTOGRAPH

General Douglas MacArthur (left), President Franklin D. Roosevelt, and Admiral Chester W. Nimitz aboard the USS Baltimore at Pearl Harbor.

creasing for a directive to the two commanders to carry out the central and southern Philippines and Formosa operations. The Navy sought to pin the Army down on the Formosa operation so that Admiral Nimitz could proceed with his planning on a firm basis. General Handy stated the Army's position on Formosa:

> We will hold off as long as we can of course but I think pretty soon we are going to have to put out some kind of a directive. [We should] put out a directive covering immediate operations, and not stick out your [the War Department's] neck on things that are not going to happen for 7 to 9 months anyhow.

The British had often used the same argument in European and Mediterranean operations. The Army's task would be to press for acceptance of the central and southern Philippines operations and to defer a decision on Formosa and Luzon until later.

In July the last U.S. Army division to be sent to the Pacific during the war arrived in Hawaii. That made twenty-one Army divisions available for deployment in the Pacific. That same month the service troop shortage was emphasized when Admiral Nimitz submitted his estimates for the Formosa operations. A shortage of more than 200,000 men, mainly service troops, would have to be met, plus additional air groups and shipping. Since SWPA would require all its service troops to support the Philippines operations and probably would also require any units that could be released from SOPAC as it rolled up its rear areas, the POA shortages would either have to be made up in POA itself, which had no surplus, or by new allocations from the United States. The difficulties in providing service troops became a major obstacle in the Navy's attempt to obtain approval of the Formosa operation.

An additional item in the Admiral's Formosa plan created interservice discussions. Suppose the planned seizure of the southwestern tip of Formosa and Amoy were not sufficient? If the Japanese were reinforced and could mount a counterattack, it might become necessary to conquer the entire island. Both General MacArthur and Admiral Nimitz were noncommittal on that point. The Army planners questioned the practicability of mounting the operation under such circumstances because a long campaign against strong enemy defenses and involving a passive population would be costly in time and casualties. The planners agreed that Formosa was a better strategic location and that initially B-29's based on Formosa could deliver a greater weight of bomb tonnage. They pointed out, however, that tactically the Philippines would be easier to take, troops could be more economically employed, and more airfields could eventually be built on Luzon. General MacArthur submitted a new set of target dates providing for the Luzon operation in February rather than April. The change also favored the Luzon operation.

Fundamentally, the provision of means was the issue in the Luzon-Formosa debate during the summer of 1944. Admiral Sherman's estimate of the service troop shortage for Formosa of over 100,000 assumed substantial help from the South Pacific. By Sept. 1 General Marshall felt that if any decision were taken then it would favor Luzon, but since other factors should be considered—the defeat of Germany—he preferred to delay making a decision. The resources released after Germany's defeat would take care of the shortages, but that defeat was still projected for the autumn of 1944. On the same date General Marshall and the Army were advised that Admiral William D. Leahy, Chief of Staff to President Roosevelt, would support the issuance of a directive that would cover operations only through Leyte.

In early September the joint planners recommended that the decision on Luzon-Formosa be made at a later date. Leyte would be invaded on Dec. 20, and preparations would be made to launch the Luzon assault on Feb. 20 or on Formosa on March 1, with the choice to be determined in the light of future events. Admiral King was unwilling to relinquish a commitment against Formosa, and he proposed a directive limiting General MacArthur to the central Philippines and giving Formosa the next priority. The Army objected, pointing out that the proposal did not state how and when the United States would take Luzon or whence the means to take Formosa would come. The shortage of service troops and the possible need of additional Army divisions indicated further demands on the Army if a decision were made to take Formosa.

Also enthusiasm was growing among Army planners that after Luzon was captured, Formosa should be bypassed and a direct assault on Japan planned. General Marshall felt a number of questions needed to be answered before a decision could be made. Admiral Leahy observed that since the United States had at that time only the means for Luzon, and since Luzon would be the least expensive operation to undertake insofar as casualties were concerned, it seemed apparent that the United States should intensify the air bombardment and sea blockade of Japan to aid the reoccupation of the Philippines.

The JSSC was given the problem for urgent consideration. The committee supported the Navy position on taking Formosa before Luzon, since it had to be taken anyway, and, if the March 1 target date was to be met, a commitment was necessary. General Marshall commented that the JSSC had in effect accepted and "made a decision" for Formosa without considering all aspects of the problem. He could not go along with the notion that postponing a decision would lengthen the war by six months, as the committee suggested, but thought that by the end of October the situation would be a great deal clearer.

Since the Army would not agree to make a package directive for Leyte and Formosa, the Navy reluctantly agreed on Sept. 8 to the issuance of a directive for Leyte along with a target date of Dec. 20. Admiral Nimitz would support the operation and plan for Formosa-Amoy on March 1 or Luzon on Feb. 20, as the case might be. After carrying out Leyte, General MacArthur would plan for the reduction of enemy air on Luzon in support of an attack on Formosa and the occupation of the northern Philippines. The two commanders-in-chief were to coordinate with each other and with CBI and the Twentieth Air Force for air support.

The acceptance by the Navy of Leyte as an objective left still unresolved the future course of operations in the Pacific after the seizure of the central Philippines. Whether U.S. forces would move against Luzon or Formosa would depend primarily on the fall of Germany and the Japanese reactions to projected carrier air strikes against the Philippines during September. Meanwhile, however, planning for both campaigns would be continued.

To Invade or Blockade Japan?

The Formosa-Luzon debates obscured an important aspect of the Pacific war as the U.S. forces advanced northward. Would Japan surrender only as a result of invasion? One group, of which Admiral Leahy was a member, felt that Japan could be strangled militarily and economically by air and sea attack and that the government would capitulate without invasion. Another group was convinced that, in the light of current experience with Japanese resistance, invasion and bitter fighting would be necessary to subdue the enemy. Still another group was undecided.

At the SEXTANT Conference in December 1943 it was the middle-of-the-road group that was responsible for the CCS decision "to obtain objectives from which . . . to invade Japan proper if this should prove necessary." When the joint planners reviewed the overall objective early in the summer of 1944, they concluded that an invasion of the industrial heart of Japan would be required to defeat Japan. The recommendation of the planners had a mixed reception. Admiral Leahy was never convinced that invasion was necessary and believed that the Navy, with some assistance from the Army Air Forces, had already defeated Japan. The JWPC felt that a conference should be held in the United States and attended by Generals MacArthur and Stilwell, Admiral Nimitz, and the Washington planners to iron out the differences of opinion on strategy.

Despite the opposition, on July 11 the JCS decided to accept the invasion objective, since defeat by bombardment and blockade would probably involve an unacceptable delay. General Marshall informed the British of their decision:

> As a result of recent operations in the Pacific, it was now clear to the U.S. Chiefs of Staff that, in order to finish the war with Japan quickly, it will be necessary to invade the industrial heart of Japan. The means for this action were not available when the over-all concept had been originally discussed. It was now, however, within our power to do this and the U.S. Chiefs of Staff feel that our intention to undertake it should be appropriately indicated.

The British agreed to the necessity for invasion on July 29, provided priority for defeating Germany was not altered, and operations would not be undertaken without CCS approval. The JCS accepted the conditions in early August.

Although the JSSC accepted the invasion as necessary, they believed that operations to make it easier should be examined and full use made of Allied ships and aircraft to avoid costly land campaigns. On Sept. 1 the JSSC was requested to make a study of the number of casualties that would be likely to occur in perimeter attacks on enemy bases as opposed to a surprise assault on the enemy homeland. In view of Saipan losses, General Marshall estimated that it would cost the United States 90,000 casualties to take Formosa, and that the high cost for that operation should be considered before rejecting the operation against Kyushu, where only one Japanese division was stationed, taking into consideration that the assault would be preceded by sustained fleet attacks.

Although there was no accurate way to estimate the loss of lives, the JSSC favored the seizure of intermediate objectives and a reduction of Japanese capabilities before a direct assault was made on the home islands. The committee favored a Formosa operation before undertaking Luzon as being less expensive in casualties, provided both were to be taken. Once Formosa was captured, the Japanese would find it more difficult to reinforce Luzon, whereas the capture of Luzon would have little effect upon Japanese capabilities to strengthen Formosa.

General Marshall's concern over the relative costs of a direct invasion as opposed to a war of attrition was shared by the other members of the JCS. Although they all wished to take the course of action that would result in the fewest casualties, they could not agree on which course that should be. Admiral Leahy felt that ultimately the President would have to decide whether to take a shorter course toward defeating Japan at a possibly greater cost in lives, or a longer course at a smaller cost. Admiral King questioned the validity of assuming that a longer war would mean fewer casualties in the end. General Marshall was impressed by Admiral Leahy's proposal that the President might have to make the final decision, but he felt that further studies of the time and loss factors should be made in the meantime.

Intelligence estimates of early September indicated that, despite heavy losses inflicted upon the Japanese air and naval forces by air bombardment and sea blockade, the Japanese land armies appeared to be not only still intact, but in fact stronger than they had been at the time of Pearl Harbor. If the fanatic and stubborn resistance shown in SWPA and CPA by Japanese troops was any indication of future opposition, actual invasion of their homeland would seem to be the only way to induce final surrender. It might have been acceptable to rely on air and naval operations to defeat Japan had there been no time element involved. The Army, however, was fully aware of the American public's distaste for long wars of attrition and it appeared to the military planners (who had no knowledge of the atom bomb in September 1944) that eventually a Pacific OVERLORD might be necessary.

Chapter VII

Postwar Political Problems

During the summer of 1944 the Allies appeared to be moving rapidly toward victory, but political pressures in the coalition war were rising in the wake of the Normandy landings. Those powerful undercurrents warned of the inevitable weakening of common bonds following a great military triumph. They were not, however, obvious to many Americans who were primarily interested in winning the war, but as time went on political questions began to take shape.

In Europe the Allied advance brought up problems of postwar settlements, including zones of occupation in Germany, and increased the interest of those Allies who had Far Eastern and Pacific possessions in the war against Japan. The defeat of Germany would end the common bond of danger in Europe that held the Allies together. The Allied nations could devote more attention to strengthening their own national security for the postwar era and achieving national goals in the war against Japan. This national self-interest complicated the Allied war effort, and the Army planners soon found themselves forced to enter more and more into the political and diplomatic fields in order to resolve the changing problems of the coalition.

The American-British Partnership

The differences between the Western Allies over ANVIL were only one aspect of the fundamental disagreement over the kind of war to fight and the objectives to be achieved by the United States and Great Britain. The American concept of the European war was to defeat Germany as quickly as possible in order to release the resources for a similar effort against Japan. It also contemplated a minimum involvement in Europe's internal affairs both during the war and afterward. Although the Army planners realized that it would be necessary to occupy Germany, that was not to be interpreted to mean that the United States would be obligated to occupy other trouble areas unless it was essential to the defeat of Germany. Such American reluctance to assume postwar responsibilities for European affairs was received by the British with considerable disappointment. Their long experience and close proximity to the Continent made them more aware that the end of a war usually means the beginning of greater responsibility.

At **SEXTANT** in November 1943 the President announced his plan for dividing Germany into several zones, and noted the desirability of American occupation of northwestern Germany. No decision was taken at the conference, and the matter was referred to the COSSAC staff for study. In its report of January 1944 the staff opposed U.S. occupation of northwestern Germany because British forces would be on the northern flank in the drive into Germany, and a change in position would necessitate administrative and logistical delay and confusion. Despite the report, the President adhered firmly to his desire that the United States should take over northwestern Germany.

In February the President spelled out his ideas on America's role in postwar Europe to Acting Secretary of State Edward R. Stettinius:

> I do not want the United States to have the post-war burden of reconstituting France, Italy, and the Balkans. This is not our natural task at a distance of 3,500 miles or more. It is definitely a British task in which the British are far more vitally interested than we are.
>
> From the point of view of the United States, our principal object is not to take part in the internal problems in southern Europe but is rather to take part in eliminating Germany as a possible and even probable cause of a third World War. . . .
>
> I have had to consider also the case of maintaining American troops in some part of Germany. . . . Therefore, I think the American policy should be to occupy northwestern Germany, the British occupying the area from the Rhine south, and also being responsible for the policing of France and Italy, if this should become necessary.
>
> In regard to the long range security of Britain against Germany, this is not a part of the first occupation. The British will have plenty of time to work that out. . . . The Americans by that time will be only too glad to retire all their military forces from Europe.

If anything further is needed to justify this disagreement with the British lines of demarcation, I can only add that political considerations in the United States make my decision conclusive.

A few days later the President wrote to the Prime Minister in a more jovial mood:

"Do please don't" ask me to keep any American forces in France. I just cannot do it! I would have to bring them all back home. As I suggested before, I denounce in protest the paternity of Belgium, France, and Italy. You really ought to bring up and discipline your own children. In view of the fact that they may be your bulwark in future days, you should at least pay for the schooling now!

The President's stand gave the Army planners firm guidance on American policy in Europe during early 1944. Backed by the President, Ambassador John G. Winant adhered to the U.S. claim for northwestern Germany before the European Advisory Commission in London during the spring of 1944. In May a directive was issued to General Eisenhower to plan for the occupation of The Netherlands and northwestern Germany, but not France, Austria, or the Balkans.

During the summer signs indicated that the President might be changing his stand and might be willing to send a token U.S. occupation force to Austria to ensure U.S. participation in its postwar administration. Despite the change in his position, the President resisted all efforts by the War and State departments to reach a compromise with the British on the German zones. The Assistant Secretary of War, John J. Clay, Secretary of State Stettinius, and Harry Hopkins sought to overcome the President's objections to U.S. occupation of a southern zone by suggesting joint control of northern Germany and Lowland ports and coordinated occupation of northern Germany. The suggestions were rejected. Roosevelt was confident he could persuade Churchill to accept his proposal, but in the meantime Army planners were preparing schemes to occupy either northwestern or southwestern Germany.

During the pursuit of German forces across France in August, General Eisenhower's decision to move Allied troops into Germany according to previous plans if Germany should collapse—the Americans in the south and the British in the north—met no objection from the Washington staff. The Army planners did not feel strongly about the question of occupation zones in Germany. What was important was the knowledge that the President intended to keep U.S. occupational responsibilities in Europe on a very limited basis territorially.

A considerable difference existed between the President's November 1943 estimate of 1,000,000 U.S. soldiers in Germany for a year or two and the Army's summer 1944 estimate of 400,000 troops at the end of a year after the defeat of Germany. Nevertheless, both estimates contemplated U.S. participation mainly in Germany and possibly the Lowlands. Anticipating public demand for some demobilization after the defeat of Germany and economy drives by Congress in the postwar period, the Army's support of the President's restricted program was understandable. The disillusioning years following World War I had not been forgotten by the War Department staff. To acquire postwar bases that could not be defended in peacetime was considered to be a liability, not an asset.

Settlement of the question of occupation zones was deferred until the President and the Prime Minister met at the OCTAGON Conference in September. In the meantime, however, the Army strategic concept of a military war as free as possible from postwar political objectives and long-range responsibilities had been given a powerful stimulant by the President. The strategic decisions to be taken in Europe and in the Pacific were influenced by the American unity on the issue. The drive to defeat the enemy as quickly and efficiently as possible was still to remain the top priority of the United States.

During the first two years of U.S. participation in the global conflict, the Pacific war was largely an American undertaking. As long as the United States recognized the primacy of the conflict in Europe, the American Army and Navy were permitted to make all the strategic decisions in the Pacific and had merely to secure the acquiescence of the British. Although periodic complaints came from the British on the buildup of resources early in the Pacific war, that growth arose out of the critical nature of the situation and the full realization that Japan had to be stopped and contained. When the enemy advance had been stopped, and the Allied counteroffensive gained momentum, the need to maintain the strategic initiative required a large increase in men, ships, and aircraft. By September 1944 there were 1,073,746 Army personnel in the Pacific, exclusive of CBI and Alaska. Such a preponderance of U.S. strength enabled the Americans to decide where and how the forces should be deployed. Disputes and arguments at the service level had generally been worked out between General Marshall and Admiral King and, with the possible exception of the Philippines, decisions had always been based upon military needs rather than political desires.

The Americans wished to preserve that status quo in the Pacific although areas existed in which other Allied nations might contribute to the war effort without prejudicing the U.S. position in the Pacific. The British could operate in the SEAC area, the Chinese in China, the Russians in Siberia and Manchuria, the French could join the British in Southeast Asia, and the Dutch, Australians, and New Zealanders could assist in SWPA. That arrangement was satisfactory while Allied forces were fighting on the Japanese perimeter. But as the island-hopping American forces defeated the Japanese and approached the more valuable overrun colonial possessions of Britain, France, and The Netherlands, those governments displayed more interest and sought to participate in decisions concerning their former territories.

During the early part of 1944, the British pressed for a greater role in the war against Japan. When the CCS met at the London conference in June 1944, the British Chiefs asked how British forces could best be employed. Since they could be based in India, the JCS recommended the Indian Ocean area as the most helpful place. As a second choice, the Americans suggested that the western flank of SWPA in the Netherlands East Indies–Malaya area might be suitable. The Americans would soon be leaving their Australian bases behind, so the British could use the bases by the time they were ready to conduct operations. Although the Americans realized that British national policy demanded that the British play a sizable role in defeating Japan, the Americans were anxious to direct those efforts into areas under British direction such as SEAC, or into General MacArthur's mixed command, rather than into the purely American setup in the Central Pacific. Any British participation would have to be self-supporting, otherwise U.S. units would have to be withdrawn from the Pacific to make room for the British on U.S. bases.

The JSSC advised the Joint Staff planners:

> In general, our strategic policy does not require either the exclusion or inclusion of the British, Russian, Dutch, or French from participation in the seizure of any enemy held territory in the Far East. The question of participation in each case should be decided solely on the basis of military consideration from the U.S. point of view.

It is compatible with our strategy to permit the reoccupation of British, French, or Dutch territories in the Far East without our military participation.

The British informed the United States in mid-July that six divisions, exclusive of Dominion troops, and a corps of two Dutch divisions would be available in 1945 if Germany were defeated by October 1944. Apparently the main and most useful contribution would still be the fleet, which would also become available in 1945. Although British forces would not be operating in the Pacific until mid-1945, General MacArthur and Admiral King wanted to keep the British out of the Netherlands East Indies unless they were under U.S. control. Both felt that it might be difficult to dislodge them once they got in. General MacArthur also believed that the British should first clean up the SEAC area and then, under his command, should help mop up in SWPA. He did not think it fair that the British should be permitted to extend SEAC boundaries later on and reap the fruits of victory in SWPA that they had done so little to merit. In his opinion it would be destructive of U.S. prestige in the Far East and would unquestionably have a most deleterious effect on future economic trends.

The British were alert to the political significance and necessity of having their forces take a prominent part in the war against Japan. In mid-August they offered their fleet for the drive into the Central Pacific. Should that be impossible, they suggested a British Empire task force with a British commander be formed to operate under General MacArthur. Of the two offers, the naval offer was the more acceptable. It was doubted that the British could spare six divisions and even if found, the U.S. would probably have to supply them. Ambassador Winant advised that the bottom of the British manpower barrel had been reached, and that demobilization was inevitable after Germany's defeat. He added that the British would have to participate in the final showdown or bad feeling might result in the postwar era.

After carefully studying the British proposals, the Army planners concluded that the British would not have much to fight with, except their navy, until the middle of 1945. By then General MacArthur should be well into the Philippines and the Allied Air Forces of SWPA and the Seventh Fleet should be "making hay" over the South China Sea. The Strategy Section pointed out that the "deployment of British forces does not involve strategy—they can neither hasten nor retard the defeat of Japan. Deployment must be based solely on high political policy." British policy was clear: "to reoccupy all British possessions where possible or to send along political officers with the occupying force; to regain their lost prestige in Australia and New Zealand; to restore French, Dutch, and Portuguese colonial possessions; and to obtain maximum U.S. aid in the political and economic reconstruction of these occupied territories."

The United States was willing to permit the return of the former possessions with the exception of Hong Kong. It wished to remain the dominant power in the Japanese mandates, the Philippines, and China. It would like to return Hong Kong and French Indochina to China, and the Philippines were to be freed, although necessary military bases would be maintained.

The Strategy Section considered that three major questions on postwar national policy had to be answered by the JCS or the President. First, did the United States want to remain the dominant power in the Southwest Pacific area? Second, did the United States want to retain any military bases in the area south of the line Solomons–French Indochina–Calcutta? If so, what? Finally, did the United States desire economic or political concessions in the Netherlands East Indies, Siam, or French Indochina? If so, then what concessions? It was concluded that until those questions were answered the problems of command, redeployment, boundaries, and divisions of responsibility could not be decided intelligently. The analysis was symptomatic of the growing importance of political elements in the strategic pattern during the summer of 1944.

Decisions on those questions could not be made overnight, but the problem of British participation required prompt attention. In September General Marshall recommended the acceptance of the British Empire task force offer. He believed that it would not interfere with General MacArthur's planned operations and that any question of logistical support could be discussed later. Apparently that failed to satisfy the British, who pressed the JCS for an answer concerning the use of their fleet in the main operations against Japan. The matter became one of the main problems to be discussed at OCTAGON.

The U.S. position with respect to Great Britain was consistent with its overall concept for a military war uncomplicated by political elements. Although the United States desired to remain apart from the internal conflicts and readjustments of Europe and the Far East, it also wished to preserve the essentially American phase of the Pacific war in the interest of speed and efficiency. In the conflict between military desirability and political expediency, the necessity for some compromise with the ambitions of the Allies appeared likely to cause some change in the American attitude.

The Russian Partner

The increasing impact of political problems in Anglo-American relations during 1944 was in direct contrast with the American-Russian relationship, which was conducted entirely on a military basis. That condition prevailed, not because the American planners were unaware that political elements were entering the situation, but because of the steadfast resistance of the President and his close advisers to any introduction of political or military bargaining with the Soviets. In light of the early sacrifices and the current successes of the Russians in their fight against Germany, some suggestions were made that the policy should be reexamined.

In February 1944 the U.S. Ambassador to Russia, W. Averell Harriman, suggested that Major General John R. Deane's military mission to the U.S.S.R. screen the Soviet requests for Lend-Lease supplies, since there no longer was a crisis. That proposal was turned down, and priorities for Lend-Lease to the U.S.S.R. remained high. Efforts to apply pressure on the Soviets to obtain some quid pro quo were ended. Although direct pressure was not favorably regarded, General Marshall pointed out to the President the following month that American aid served a useful purpose in itself:

> An important factor enabling the Soviets to seize the offensive and retain it is Lend-Lease. Lend-Lease food and transport particularly have been vital factors in Soviet success. Combat aircraft, upon which the Soviet Air Forces relied so greatly, have been furnished in relatively great numbers (11,-300 combat planes received). Should there be a full stoppage it is extremely doubtful whether Russia could retain efficiently her all-out offensive capabilities. Even defensively the supply of Lend-Lease food and transport would play an extremely vital role. It amounts to about a million tons a year. If Russia were deprived of it, Germany could probably still defeat the USSR. Lend-Lease is our trump card in dealing with USSR and its control is possibly the most effective means we have to keep the Soviets on the offensive in connection with the second front.

Thus, the possibility that Lend-Lease might be curtailed or cut off was recognized as a weapon to ensure Soviet cooperation with OVERLORD.

In May 1944 the JCS attempted to establish a policy on Lend-Lease following the defeat of Germany that would limit U.S. aid exclusively to those Allied forces employed against Japan. But after a delay of four months they were informed that the President would make such national policy decisions himself.

Since the military staff was unable to employ its most potent weapon in dealing with the Russians, it was forced to handle Soviet requests purely on a military basis. In April General Deane (chief of the U.S. military mission to the U.S.S.R.) recommended conditioning U.S. approval of Soviet petitions for heavy bombers and C-54 transport aircraft upon Soviet reciprocity in the matter of bases for U.S. bombers to be used against Japan. The AAF advised him that bomber buildup and training time would preclude any use by the Soviets of a bomber force before the spring of 1945. Since the United States was planning to reduce aircraft production as soon as possible, and since current production estimates would not support the development of a Soviet bomber force that would be of little value in defeating Germany, it did not seem wise to the AAF to grant the request. The AAF also pointed out that the Russians would probably demand special equipment for the bombers that was not only still in short supply, but also had not been released for use by America's other Allies.

Although the Army was not disposed to build up a Soviet bomber force, it was quite willing to impress the Russians with the technical capabilities of the AAF bomber forces. In an endeavor to improve U.S.–Soviet relations during the fall of 1943 and enable Allied aircraft to bomb targets beyond their radius of action and so subject the entire German Reich to long-range air attack, the Army Air Forces had proposed a shuttle-bombing project (FRANTIC) from bases in the U.K., Italy, and the U.S.S.R. Such an operation would demonstrate the solidarity of the three partners and would help to obtain use of Siberian bases later in the war against Japan.

Although Premier Stalin had approved the proposal at Tehran, it took several months of negotiations before three bases in the Ukraine—Poltava, Mirgorod, and Piryatin—were selected and made usable. Major General Ira C. Eaker led the first mission from the Mediterranean to the Russian bases on June 2. The Soviets were suspicious of foreigners on their soil and insisted on establishing a complicated procedure of group visas for U.S. airmen landing in

Russia. The Soviets evinced some reluctance to permitting the U.S. bombers to attack major strategic targets, yet despite a disastrous German night raid on the shuttle bases on June 21–22, seven missions were flown during the summer.

As the Allied forces swept toward Germany during that period, some objectives were eliminated as targets, whereas others came within range of the fighter and bomber aircraft operating from bases in France and Italy. As the military necessity for shuttle bombing ended, the Soviets indicated that they wished to terminate the project. Their reason was the limitation caused by the approaching winter weather. The Americans wanted to retain the Ukraine bases, and General Eaker suggested that the United States place some restrictions on Soviet air operations in the Mediterranean-Balkans area in order to change the Soviet position. His suggestion received scant encouragement in Washington.

The Polish uprising against the Germans in Warsaw on Aug. 1 led to the last shuttle-bombing mission. The Russians were very close to Warsaw at the time, but they made no move to aid the beleaguered Poles and even denounced the leaders of the revolt as reckless adventurers. Appeals by the President and Prime Minister for aid to the Poles made little impression on the Soviet Premier. Finally on Sept. 11 he approved an American airdrop of supplies into Warsaw. An airdrop was made on Sept. 18, but with inadequate supplies and practically no hope of relief, the insurrectionists surrendered about two weeks later. The collapse of the Polish revolt was followed by the closing of the shuttle bases. By Nov. 1 only a small caretaker detachment remained at Poltava, and the other two had been vacated.

Considerable debate has taken place as to the value of FRANTIC. It did result in some U.S.–Soviet air collaboration, and it served to display U.S. technical superiority. The strategic achievements are less discernible, and except for the heavy night raid on June 21–22, the Germans paid little attention to the project. Many of the objectives of the FRANTIC missions could have been attacked from the U.K. or the Mediterranean, and by the time the first shuttle mission was flown the Allies were just about to demonstrate their good faith to the Soviets by the Normandy landings.

Perhaps the political experience gained by the American military and civilian negotiators in their efforts to maintain the operation was the most valuable result of the FRANTIC operation. Despite frequent Russian opposition, they managed to get seven missions approved. That was quite a feat in itself, as the Russians had resisted all other efforts to introduce foreign troops to Soviet territory. At this point in time, one wonders why the Russians ever consented to it.

During the summer of 1944 the Army planners recognized the need for closer liaison with the Russians in regard to the conclusion of the European war and to the association of the U.S.S.R. in the Japanese conflict. Despite their promises to enter the war against Japan, the Russians had made no military commitments in the Far East. The United States was trying to keep the British out of the Pacific on one hand and trying to lure the Russians in on the other. General Arnold observed that the U.S.S.R. had no intention of fighting a two-front war and kept all negotiations in the planning stage. Little progress had been made in getting the Russians to plan concretely in the Far East despite Premier Stalin's pledge at SEXTANT to enter the Far East conflict as soon as Germany was defeated.

U.S. officers were permitted to inspect Siberian ports—wearing civilian clothing to prevent a Japanese protest—but information on the availability, location, and condition of airfields in the maritime provinces, and the logistical implications of supplying those bases, were hung up in a mass of Soviet indifference and red tape, notwithstanding a personal plea by the President to the Premier in August. The possible use of the northern route against Japan was still being considered by the joint planners, but the casual attitude of the Soviet authorities suggested that nothing would be done to excite Japanese fears or resentment until the end of the European war.

It was still a moot question in the summer of 1944 whether the U.S.S.R. would be essential to the defeat of Japan. The joint planners believed that Japanese capitulation would not depend on active participation of the U.S.S.R., since Soviet capabilities would be limited for some months after Germany's defeat. But a member of the JSSC felt that the entry of the Soviet Union would be "of most cardinal importance" in holding down the Japanese Kwantung army on the mainland if the United States invaded Japan. No agreement existed among the U.S. leaders on the need for an invasion of Japan, and the U.S.S.R.'s value in the Pacific war depended on an assault on Japan. Siberia would be helpful but not essential for air bases from which to strike Japanese military and industrial targets. However, when the JCS accepted the need for an invasion for planning purposes, the desire was stimulated to obtain closer cooperation with the Russians and to begin active planning for the day when the U.S.S.R. would join in the war against Japan.

The U.S. military mission in Moscow reported that the opposition to Soviet planning on air matters was from political sources, not from the Soviet Army or Air Staff. An obvious effort was made by Soviet authorities to avoid all air collaboration: in September, after six weeks, there were still no replies to the U.S. Far Eastern base proposals. Ambassador Harriman and his military mission made another effort to have pressure applied on the Russians to obtain consideration for American requests. But, like its predecessor, that plea was also disapproved.

By the middle of September, U.S.–Soviet military affairs concerning the Japanese war were still submerged in unanswered requests. Administrative delay, the familiar explanation of the British in Burma, had a counterpart in the Soviet position in the Far East.

The French Relationship

The French attitude was quite the opposite of that of the Soviet Union. France was eager to participate on as large a scale as possible in the European and Far Eastern wars. The desire to restore French prestige and national pride made the leaders of the French forces eager to rebuild their armed forces and to play an active and important role in the defeat of Germany and Japan. France could ill afford to have its possessions returned as a gift, thus losing face in the Far East. Moreover, unless French forces were able to strike back hard at their German conquerors, French national morale might be seriously affected, and postwar recovery might be made more difficult.

Being oriented to conducting an efficient military war, the joint planners were not overly enthusiastic about the plans presented by the Washington representatives of the French Committee of National Liberation (FCNL) in late 1943 for raising and equipping new French divisions. Time and production factors were already operating against any increases in the French rearmament program that could not be fully justified as contributing to the defeat of Germany. General Marshall pointed out to the JCS in November 1943 that the question of rearming more than the eleven divisions already approved at Casablanca was a matter of national policy and should be decided by the President on the basis of its postwar implications.

The French rearmament problem was further complicated during early 1944 by the involved relations between the Americans and British on one hand and the French Committee of National Liberation on the other. The President was reluctant to reorganize the committee as the provisional government of France, and he was determined to stay out of French postwar problems. The President instructed General Eisenhower in March that the defeat of Germany was his first aim, but he desired that democratic methods be fostered during the coming liberation of France so that favorable conditions could be established for the eventual formation of a representative French government. He refused to deal with the FCNL on a political level and insisted that any discussions regarding the future employment of the existing French forces be carried on with General Eisenhower.

Since the President was not disposed to support the authority of the FCNL and General Charles de Gaulle, additional problems developed during the spring. Misunderstandings arose over the supplying of the French resistance groups and over the issuance of invasion currency for OVERLORD forces. The British and Americans had little confidence in French security measures; consequently the French leaders were told little of the details of OVERLORD until the last possible moment. Very likely these were contributing factors to the failure of the negotiations to have General de Gaulle broadcast an appeal to the French people on D Day for their cooperation with OVERLORD. The General's visit to Washington in early July clarified the situation somewhat, but the role of the French forces in the liberation of France and in the defeat of Germany remained vague and uncertain.

In spite of the political impasse, General Marshall endeavored to keep the question of French rearmament on a military basis. General Marshall instructed the Joint Logistics Committee in late July on considering French requests for rearming more divisions, stating:

> The Chief of Staff desires that an answer to all these questions (rearmament, French air forces, resistance groups, civilian labor) be arrived at which will utilize the available French manpower in a well-balanced fighting force to include the normal components of combat support troops and service troops with the necessary headquarters, consistent with manpower limitations, and solely with this objective: the utilization of French manpower as effectively as is possible in order to prosecute the war to a rapid conclusion. In other words, no consideration should be given, by any committee, to the development of a postwar French Army; only those troops should be equipped and armed who can participate in the war at an early date.

That military approach to the French rearmament problem was further reflected by the British in their proposal to the JCS and the State Department in late August. The British suggested that, in the immediate postwar period, they would be responsible for equipping the forces of Belgium, Holland, Denmark, and Norway, and the United States would take care of France. They stated that thus the forces of those nations could be closely integrated with those of the United States and Great Britain. In passing the proposal to committees for staff action, the JCS cautioned that it was a postwar matter and that the U.S. Chiefs should make no commitments without Presidential approval.

Initial reaction to the British suggestion was unfavorable. The Joint Logistics Committee concluded that the plan might foster spheres of influence that might restrict operations of U.S. manufacturers after the war. In addition to rearming the French, the development of a closely related Western European bloc would exclude the U.S.S.R. and would oppose a strong international organization. The JLC suggested that the plan be discussed with the Soviets on a tripartite basis. The committee also recommended expanding the plan to include all liberated nations rather than just the Western European countries.

The Joint Strategic Survey Committee disagreed in part with the recommendations of the JLC. The JSSC believed that rearming Western European Allies would permit the United States to reduce and then withdraw its occupational forces in Europe at earlier dates. The JSSC favored the British proposal conditionally, but they also agreed with the JLC that any implication of U.S. encouragement of a Western bloc should be avoided, and that the U.S.S.R. should be consulted.

While the French rearmament and postwar forces were being examined, Allied forces had swept across France, and thousands of eligible Frenchmen were made available for wartime duty. The questions of how many could be used and how best to use them bothered the Allies for the rest of the summer. If Germany were defeated in the early fall of 1944, as was then expected, there would be no requirement for additional French combat divisions, but there would be a need for service, garrison, and line-of-communications troops. If, however, the war continued into 1945, then more French divisions could be very helpful. Therefore a decision on the problem would have to be postponed until the tactical situation became clearer, and the Allies could estimate the amount and kind of help they wanted from France.

The French also approached the CCS on the matter of their future participation in the war against Japan. Naturally their chief interest was Indochina, just as the Dutch and Portuguese were voicing concern about their colonial possessions in the Pacific. Those nations wished to regain their territories from the Japanese; and the British, who had a similar interest in the Pacific, supported their efforts.

The political importance of helping France and other nations with colonial possessions was obvious to the Army planners. As in the case of the British, they saw no reason to object to the recovery of prewar possessions, provided no U.S. forces were involved in the process. The Army planners did not wish to incur the future enmity of native populations by allowing American soldiers to assist in the resubjugation of colonies, especially when the prospect of a rise in Asiatic nationalism, sparked by Japanese wartime propaganda, was likely to follow the close of hostilities. In the days ahead the United States would have to face the problem of keeping its aid on a military basis and warding off any political stigma.

U.S. Problems with Other Nations

The desire of the United States to become involved in Europe's political affairs only to the extent necessary to defeat Germany was apparent not only in its relations with the great powers in Europe, but also in its dealings with smaller nations during the summer of 1944. The Army planners were especially cautious regarding the Balkans. Supported by the President's pronouncement on shunning U.S. postwar commitments in that area, the planners regarded the various proposals with wariness.

In April General Marshall had advised the JCS that he felt that equipping patriot forces in the Balkans for wartime use against the Germans was justified, but that there should be no complete rearming for postwar conditions. The Operations Division had recommended that U.S. participation in civil affairs in Albania, Yugoslavia, and Greece be limited to relief and rehabilitation; and that in regard to Austria, Hungary, Bulgaria, and Rumania, American participation be contingent upon actual employment of U.S. forces in those countries. The JCS agreed with that recommendation and informed the British in late May that no U.S. forces would be employed in southern Europe on occupational duty, and that any remaining in the area at the end of the war would be withdrawn as soon as practicable. That disavowal of U.S. responsibility in the Balkans was supported by the American position on ANVIL versus Italian operations and the Balkans during the summer and proved to be one of the sore spots in Anglo-American relations for the rest of the war. Thus, it left the question of Balkan leadership to be settled between the British and the Soviets, although the President thought he should still be consulted on any arrangements that were to be made.

The role of Turkey—which was associated with the Balkan issue in many ways—came up for discussion in July. As the war had progressed, the military necessity for Turkish entry on the Allied side had also diminished. The Russians were inclined to attach less importance to Turkish participation, and the joint planners agreed with them. Strategically, Turkish forces could be used only against Bulgaria, and the Army staff was well aware that the U.S.S.R had special interests in Bulgaria. The Strategy Section therefore concluded that it would be better to have Turkey stay out of the war. The United States would have to provide technicians and equipment, which would require the use of critical shipping. If the Turks were to attack Bulgaria, Soviet forces would be brought into the southern Balkans, and neither the British nor the Turks wanted that to occur. The Strategy Section maintained that if the Germans evacuated Greece, the United States could distribute its forces in the Mediterranean to allow the British to occupy Greece; but if the Germans did not, then no diversion should be made.

Fundamentally the planners believed the question of American support of British policy in the Mediterranean was a long-range decision that should be made primarily on the basis of whether the United States would need to retain a close Anglo-American alliance after the war. If close alliance was desirable, safeguarding the British lines of communications in the Mediterranean should be assured.

Despite the various disadvantages and alternatives to Turkish entry into the war, both the JCS and the State Department decided that Turkey should be encouraged to sever diplomatic relations with Germany as quickly as possible as a first step toward belligerency. The approval included certain important provisions: that the United States would not commit itself to support a campaign in the Balkans and would not divert resources from agreed operations in the western Mediterranean. The United States was forced to modify its position in early August when the Turks expressed their concern over such a conditional approval. If a Balkan campaign should develop, the United States agreed to reconsider the matter and to determine if portions of Turkish requests for aid could be made available.

The Army planners were well aware of the unsettled conditions in the Balkan-Aegean area and the possibility of a Soviet clash with the British if their interests conflicted. In September the Strategy Section pointed out that the United States might be placed in the middle by ensuing circumstances, and Germany's hope of creating dissension among the Allies in order to obtain more lenient peace terms might be realized. The Balkan problems and the dispute with the Soviet Union over the relief of Warsaw made the potential for deepening rifts seem even more acute. The Army staff was unable to do anything about the situation, but it was another factor to be considered in future planning.

The military staff's problems were not limited to the political and military areas, but they also included diplomatic matters pertaining to European neutrals. Foreign nationals were primarily the concern of the State Department, but the trading of vital military materials to Germany by Sweden, Switzerland, Turkey, and Portugal had been a troublesome problem to the Army for a long time. Robert P. Patterson, Undersecretary of War, recommended in June that the State Department discontinue applying gradual pressure on those neutral countries and insist that they stop supplying the enemy. Secretary Cordell Hull replied that the United States had to act in concert with the British in those matters, and that some reduction in Swedish ball-bearing exports had already been arranged. Later, Sweden turned down a British-American demand, which was supported by the U.S.S.R., for a change in policy with Sweden. Secretary Hull then suggested that the threat of taking control of Swedish interests in the United States might be used to apply additional pressure. Allied insistence upon further reductions in Swedish trade with Germany, added to the threat of postwar commercial disadvantages to Sweden should it continue such trade, resulted in a change in Swedish policy in late 1944, when their export trade with Germany was terminated.

A different problem was presented by Switzerland, which did not possess Sweden's resources. In July General Marshall informed the CCS that the United States did not want the Swiss to use war materials imported from the Allies to supply Germany. Although the British appreciated the American position, they did not favor such strong measures as cutting off exports to Switzerland. They favored using persuasion and increased political pressure. Basically, the problem of trading with the enemy by Switzerland and other neutral countries depended upon the short-term military advantages over a severe Allied economic policy, as opposed to long-term economic disadvantages and resentment against the Allies that the neutral countries might carry over into the postwar period.

The Army planners were well aware of the political implications involved in many of the matters brought to their attention, but they received little guidance or encouragement from the President to concern themselves with the problems. The continuity of coordination in those problems between the War Department and the State Department left something to be desired. Neither department could be entirely faulted for such lack of coordination as it was frequently difficult to obtain a decision from the President, who preferred to handle his own foreign affairs.

Lacking top-level positive political guidance, the Army planners often resorted to its general guideline in making decisions: Would a given proposal help to end the war more quickly and efficiently? The attainment of postwar objectives, with the exception of certain Army and Army Air Force bases, was not within the Army province. As a result, some of the courses of action endorsed by the Army planners during that period may appear to have been shortsighted. If so, it was because the military staff felt duty-bound to limit its considerations to military aspects of the matter, but not because they were unaware of possible long-range political effects.

In the summer of 1944 there was no doubt that from a military viewpoint, the Army had been successful in conducting the war. The accelerated progress in Europe and in the Pacific provided ample evidence of the soundness of its strategic concept. The forthcoming conference at Quebec would confirm the satisfaction with the military course of the war felt by the British and American delegates. Irrespective of the disturbing political problems, the defeat of Germany was in sight and, to the Army staff, a military victory was the primary goal.

Chapter VIII

OCTAGON, the Second Quebec Conference

During the summer of 1944 the German position deteriorated steadily. The OVERLORD and ANVIL-DRAGOON drives had brought the Western Allied forces to the German border. In Italy, Allied troops had penetrated the Pisa-Rimini line. In the east the Russians had moved into Poland and the Baltic states. The German satellites—Rumania, Bulgaria, and Finland—had defected, and the three fronts were converging. Although no significant signs of internal collapse were discernible, intelligence estimates indicated that a German surrender would occur by Dec. 1 at the latest.

By the end of summer General MacArthur's forces had control over most of New Guinea, and Admiral Nimitz had seized the southern Marianas. While the conference was in progress, SWPA troops assaulted Morotai, and POA forces landed in the southern Palaus. The encircling Allied lines were drawing ever closer about Japan. Only in CBI was the situation disturbing as the Japanese moved in on American airfields in eastern China, but the favorable Allied progress in northern Burma and the increasing airlift tonnage to China were sources of some comfort.

The OCTAGON Conference

In the flush of success and forthcoming victory, Anglo-American conferees assembled in Quebec on Sept. 12 for the series of discussions fostered by the British. The second Quebec conference convened in the impressive Château Frontenac, high on the north bank of the St. Lawrence River. It was there that, after considering the Allied string of victories in Europe and the Pacific, Prime Minister Churchill asserted "Everything we had touched had turned to gold. . . ."

123

The U.S. attendance at the five-day conference was limited to the four Joint Chiefs of Staff, two of the Joint Strategic Survey Committee, the four Joint Staff Planners, three chiefs of operations, two JCS secretaries, and twenty-two planning officers, a total of thirty-seven. The Americans had consented to the conference reluctantly, feeling that strategically there was relatively little to discuss. It was only because of repeated requests from Churchill that the President agreed to meet him and the CCS in another full-scale conference.

Considering how well the Allied forces were functioning in Europe, it was apparent that the tactical strategy should be left to the field commanders. Further, the Americans were not interested in discussing Pacific strategy at that time. The absence of urgent military issues signified that the conference might well be concerned with political questions. To prepare for such an occurrence, the Chief of Staff was briefed by the Operations Division on the two items deemed to be most urgent to the British: the U.S. proposal to withdraw the Fifth Army from Italy to France, and the British proposal to join in the Pacific war.

The Operations Division believed that if the Fifth Army could be used effectively in France, then all or part of it should be transferred there. The timing of the transfer would depend on the progress of the offensive in Italy. If General Eisenhower could not use the Fifth Army in France, it should be employed in a campaign toward Vienna rather than permitting it to become committed to Balkan operations. The army planners did not object to the British engaging in operations in southeastern Europe so long as agreed plans were not jeopardized. If it were possible, the United States should consider supporting the British in the Balkans with shipping and transport planes. The unwillingness to have U.S. troops involved in the Balkans was similar to that in the colonial areas in the Far East. Again, the planners felt that on a long-term basis little good and considerable harm might result.

The British were assured by General Marshall that the United States did not propose to withdraw the Fifth Army from Italy until General Wilson had completed the campaign then being conducted to defeat Generalfeldmarshal Albert Kesselring. Now that DRAGOON had been successfully launched, the U.S. Joint Chiefs of Staff were more sympathetic to a British amphibious landing on the Istrian Peninsula. Admiral King announced his willingness to permit General Wilson to use the amphibious landing craft employed in the southern France operation should he decide to carry out the plan sponsored by the British. Since shipping was also required

U.S. ARMY PHOTOGRAPH

President Franklin D. Roosevelt and Prime Minister Winston Churchill review Guard of Honor at The Citadel upon arrival for Quebec Conference. At left may be seen the Château Frontenac, where military discussions took place.

elsewhere, the CCS agreed to give General Wilson until Oct. 10 to make up his mind on the operation. From a U.S. standpoint, a British attack against the Istrian Peninsula would probably be followed by a drive toward Vienna, which would be likely to avoid the controversial Balkans and bring additional pressure on Germany.

Other European matters discussed presented no conflict. The CCS agreed that command of the forces in southern France should pass from General Wilson to General Eisenhower on Sept. 15, and they found little fault with General Eisenhower's expressed intention of striking through the West Wall into the Ruhr and Saar. His plan to make the main effort in the north was approved, and the CCS seconded his desire to open the ports of Antwerp and Rotterdam before poor weather conditions set in.

At the British suggestion, the strategic bombing effort was brought back under the CCS, with General Arnold and Air Chief Marshal Sir Charles Portal acting as executive agents. The principal reason for the change was to restore to more direct control of the Air Ministry the British bombers under Air Chief Marshal Sir Arthur Harris, who had been operating closely with General Eisenhower's staff. The change had little effect on American operations, which continued to be carried out by coordination between General Eisenhower and Lieutenant General Carl A. Spaatz, commander of U.S. Strategic Air Forces in Europe.

Since the CCS lacked the authority to settle the question of occupation zones in Germany, they sought guidance from the President and the Prime Minister. Theretofore the President had resisted all efforts to arrange a compromise, but suddenly the President reversed himself and agreed to accept the original COSSAC proposal that British forces should occupy northwestern Germany and U.S. forces southwestern Germany. Soviet forces were to control the eastern portion, and Berlin would be administered under a tripartite control arrangement.

It is not clear what influenced the President's decision. Churchill suggests in his book, *Triumph and Tragedy*, that by OCTAGON the President had become persuaded by the U.S. and British arguments to accept the southwestern zone. Admiral Leahy recalled that "after tedious argument with Prime Minister Churchill he [the President] accepted the British contention that Northwest Germany would be of more value to the future of our friend and ally England than to the United States of America." However, by OCTAGON the President had learned of the British intention to assume responsibility for southeastern Europe and Austria and of the practicability of supplying U.S. forces in southern Germany via the Low Countries and northern Germany. Perhaps those developments tended to remove the President's objection. The Morgenthau Plan, which was accepted at OCTAGON, may also have influenced the President's decision.

To help the United States solve its logistical problems, the British agreed to let Bremen and its port, Bremerhaven, come under U.S. control. The arrangement was in accord with General Eisenhower's tactical plans, since the British on the north and the Americans on the south would be in or close to their zones of occupation when Germany surrendered. It also eliminated the necessity of a postwar transfer of armed forces and numerous complications occasioned by such a transfer.

Future measures to prevent the rearmament of Germany were also discussed by the President and the Prime Minister. Churchill stated that the British would want to be quite harsh with the nation that had caused them to go through two terrible wars. The two heads of government considered dismantling the war-making industries of the Ruhr and the Saar under the aegis of some world organization as a possible solution. They initialed the so-called Morgenthau (Henry J., Secretary of the Treasury) Plan, which would eliminate the heavy industry in those areas and would foster a return of Germany to an agricultural economy. Secretary Morgenthau commented shortly after the OCTAGON conference that the President withheld his consent to an American occupation of a southwestern zone in Germany because he wanted the British to be charged with implementation of the Morgenthau Plan in the Ruhr and Saar areas in the northern zone.

The Prime Minister also brought up the subject of continuing Lend-Lease aid to the British. The President agreed that Britain must rebuild its export trade if it were once more to pay its way after the war. He also believed it would be proper not to attach any conditions to future Lend-Lease that might jeopardize Britain's recovery. He was assured by Churchill that no U.S. goods thus acquired would be exported or sold for profit.

In order to secure closer Soviet cooperation in Europe and the Far East the conferees decided to establish a combined military committee in Moscow to represent the Chiefs of Staff of the Big Three on strategy and operational matters. The U.S. and British military heads of mission in the U.S.S.R. would act for the CCS, and it was hoped that the Russians would appoint a senior General Staff officer to the committee. However, the familiar delaying tactics on the part of the Russians followed, and the committee was never established.

With the collapse of Germany expected in the near future, more attention was given to the war against Japan. The enemy's position had become considerably more difficult, although the war in the Pacific was far from over. Intelligence estimates reported that Japanese aircraft production had increased, but that heavy air losses had resulted in a serious shortage of trained pilots and crews. The Japanese Navy and merchant marine had sustained severe losses at sea, and the shipping outlook was critical. Thereafter, the Japanese Navy and Air Force would be committed only when the "Inner Zone" was menaced or attacked. The intelligence estimate of the enemy situation also reported that only the Japanese ground forces remained intact and capable of bitter and prolonged resistance.

In the attempt to recapture the Philippines, U.S. forces would soon be approaching the "Inner Zone," and severe land battles appeared to lie ahead. Although the Army planners were sure of final victory, their confidence was tempered by a feeling of caution and anxiety that stemmed from the conflicting desires to speed up the war and to hold down casualties. The invasion concept was accepted during the summer of 1944 and confirmed at OCTAGON. The Army planners would therefore be occupied in finding courses of action that would be acceptable, as to speed and casualties, to the military authorities and to the American public.

In their search the planners got a helping hand from Admiral Halsey's fleet carriers and Army Air Forces units under General Kenney. In sweeps over the Philippines in early September, Third Fleet aircraft caused great Japanese losses and destruction that followed the devastating air strikes of the Army Air Forces. The lack of air opposition caused Admiral Halsey to suggest that the Palaus operation be canceled, and that forces scheduled for the operations be assigned to General MacArthur for an immediate assault upon Leyte. Here was a real demonstration of the doctrine of flexibility, but a quick exchange of messages between Admirals Halsey and Nimitz, General MacArthur, and the JCS at Quebec revealed that the plan was a bit too daring. Admiral Halsey's superiors still felt that the Palaus were necessary to further advance, but they were willing to cancel the Yap operation and release three Army divisions to General MacArthur. It took only ninety minutes to secure the approval of the JCS, and the target date for Leyte was advanced two entire months to Oct. 20. Also, all intermediate operations after Morotai were canceled.

As the Navy and Army Air Forces increased the tempo of their operations, the war in the Pacific moved ahead rapidly. That may have been one of the reasons the British took a firm position at the conference on their future role in the main operations against Japan. The British had large political and economic stakes in the Far East, and they also realized that a military victory was essential to remove the psychological effects of their defeat in 1941–42. Although Churchill firmly opposed bypassing Singapore, the President suggested it might be too strongly garrisoned by the Japanese. Churchill argued that a campaign to recapture Singapore would engage large enemy forces, help the U.S. Pacific drive, and yield a "grand prize." The capture of Singapore would probably occur too late to affect the outcome of the war against Japan, but the humiliating loss of 1942 had to be redeemed militarily by the British to bolster their prestige in the Far East for the postwar era.

Since the President provided no guidance on any future plans he may have had in mind for Hong Kong and Indochina, the Army planners abstained from committing any U.S. forces for political purposes. Although the recapture of the Philippines had political overtones, the Philippines were a valuable military target and would have to be taken in any event.

Although the United States was willing to accept the participation of other interested Allies in the war against Japan and to acquiesce in the recovery of former possessions, a bitter CCS debate developed at OCTAGON over the size and area of British contribution. The British wished to put their main fleet in the Pacific under Admiral Nimitz instead of using it to clear the Indian Ocean or to harry the enemy's flank in the Malaya–Netherlands East Indies sector. The British felt that for political reasons they must make a good showing in the operation against the Japanese homeland. Admiral King, however, saw no reason to withdraw U.S. naval units to make room for British forces when they were not needed and, in his opinion, could be used more profitably elsewhere. The fact that the President had twice accepted the Prime Minister's flat offer of the British fleet made Admiral King's position difficult to uphold, but he refused to make any definite arrangements on the use of British naval units. In the end, the CCS agreed that a balanced and self-supporting British fleet would participate in the main Pacific operations and that its employment would be decided from time to time in accordance with prevailing circumstances. The British withdrew their alternative offer to form an Empire task force, since acceptance of the fleet had been their preferred proposal.

General Arnold was similarly unhappy about the British offer of very long-range bomber assistance, which the British made for the first time at OCTAGON. The conferees agreed that Air Marshal Portal should prepare for planning purposes an estimate of the possible RAF contribution in the war against Japan. The British had succeeded in getting their fleet into the Pacific, at least on paper, but the vague terminology of the agreement foreshadowed additional debate. General Marshall remained somewhat aloof from the debate since the Army's interests were not directly involved. When he did take part, he was more of an intermediary than a partisan.

The JCS were not enthusiastic over British interest in the Pacific, but they were in complete agreement with their ally's desire to conclude the Burma commitment as quickly as possible. If the British were to participate in other SEAC operations and recapture Singapore, they would first have to defeat the enemy in Burma and free the forces and resources engaged there. The Rangoon operation would require about six divisions, which would have to be pulled out of Italy and northwestern Europe. Since that transfer depended on the progress of the war in Europe, any action on Rangoon would be out of the question until at least the spring of 1945. Lord Mountbatten would try in the meantime to advance in the direction of Mandalay with the aid of the Ledo and Yunnan Chinese forces. Land communication with China would be opened as soon as possible and the air route secured.

If the Rangoon operation could not be carried out early in 1945, then the Mandalay advance would be exploited as far as possible. Prime Minister Churchill asked for two divisions from the United States to assist the British in Burma. General Marshall turned down the request, stating that every division in the United States was already allocated either to Europe or to the Pacific.

The British proposal that, in planning for the defeat of Japan, a date of two years after the defeat of Germany be used for the redeployment of forces, planning of production, and allocation of manpower, was not acceptable to the JCS. General Marshall advised the British Chiefs of Staff that the U.S. Army used a time factor of one year for redeployment and demobilization, but that for planning of production and allocation of manpower, a compromise estimate of eighteen months would be satisfactory. The CCS adopted the U.S. suggestion and made arrangements for the periodic adjustments of this time element in the light of progress of the war. The CCS also decided that there should be combined exploration into the problems of redeployment and available shipping for the period following the end of the war in Europe.

In the operational area, the British approved the U.S. program of Pacific objectives for 1944–45. During the conference the schedule was changed when the date of the Leyte assault was advanced. General Arnold reported that B-29's of the Twentieth Air Force were operating from China but that they would soon be able to operate from the Marianas and would be able to bomb the Japanese homeland. As airfields became available, additional B-29 groups would be based on Luzon or Formosa.

Toward the end of the conference General Marshall suggested that a press statement be issued by the President and the Prime Minister characterizing the tenor of the meetings:

> . . . the only difficulty encountered at the conference was the problem of providing employment for all the Allied forces who were eager to participate in the war against Japan. The difficulty had arisen as a result of the keenness of the competition to employ the maximum possible forces for the defeat of Japan.

The fact that there were few and relatively minor disagreements appeared to indicate the summit of coalition warfare and the "golden era" of combined strategic planning. Although no important decisions were made—and from a military viewpoint it might just as well have not been held—the conference was the forerunner of the political meetings at Yalta and Potsdam. The Prime Minister was very concerned about "the political dangers of divergencies" between the Soviet Union and the Western Allies with respect to Poland, Greece, and Yugoslavia, but his proposal to "add a word" to this effect to the communication to Premier Stalin summarizing the military results of the conference was turned down by the President. All signs pointed unmistakably to fuller discussions and profound considerations of political problems in the near future. Common military problems would become increasingly dwarfed by the rise of national interests and international policy conflicts. From then on the problems of winning the war would come up against the problems of winning the peace.

OCTAGON was the last of the midwar conferences, and in some ways it was reminiscent of the first in the series—the Casablanca Conference of January 1943. Both conferences were inconclusive, but they marked a transition from one era to another. Casablanca initiated the predominantly military conferences of 1943–44, and OCTAGON was the first of the predominantly political meetings that would typify the last year of the war. In January 1943 no accepted overall plan had existed for the defeat of Germany, and strategy had been conducted on an opportunistic basis, best illustrated by the decision to invade Sicily. By September 1944 the Allies were in the same position with respect to Japan—flexibility was the keynote, and timing of the operations was sometimes made on the spur of the moment, the Leyte decision, for example. At Casablanca the CCS were interested in the possible effects of the Combined Bomber Offensive on Germany. At Quebec the influence of the B-29's on the Japanese was given similar attention. One of the problems that had been given great attention at Casablanca was the ANAKIM operation to clear Burma of the Japanese. After many variations during the ensuing period, a full cycle had been completed, and at OCTAGON an operation to drive the enemy from Burma was back on the planning books.

Some points of contrast between the two conferences symbolized the attainment of maturity by the U.S. planning staffs and their functioning as well as the progress of the war. U.S. staff preparations for the international conferences had been reduced practically to a science. The elaborate compilations of background data to brief the Chief of Staff and his assistants fully were carefully prepared in advance. The Americans had learned the British committee procedure well and could now meet their Allies on an equal basis. It was a far cry from the inexperience of the overtaxed staff at the Casablanca Conference. The U.S. staff and its chiefs had drawn much closer to the President in planning for military operations. As a result they were able to present and maintain a united front in their debates and discussions with the British. Unfortunately, similar White House–military staff coordination was still lacking on political matters.

A number of basic concepts had also changed materially during the interval between the two conferences. China's importance had been so modified that it was a mere shadow of its former position, whereas the hope that the U.S.S.R. would enter the war against Japan had been strengthened immeasurably. The elaborate scheming of the Allies to induce Turkey to enter the war against Germany had become of very secondary importance. In fact, no mention was made of Turkey at OCTAGON. The Mediterranean issue, too, which was greatly debated at Casablanca, received little attention at Quebec. Yet the guarded optimism at Casablanca that Japan

U.S. ARMY PHOTOGRAPH

At Casablanca, President Roosevelt and Prime Minister Churchill quietly read their joint communiqué, their high-ranking Army and Navy officials in background, during week of Jan. 17, 1943.

might not have to be invaded had been replaced by the grim assumption that invasion of the enemy's homeland was inevitable. The Americans had sounded an offensive note against Japan at Casablanca, but the conservative and somewhat defensive attitude at Casablanca on the war in the Far East had been superseded by a more offensive audacious spirit at OCTAGON. Speed had become part of the U.S. strategic concept, and the British, who at Casablanca had been reluctant to countenance any major Pacific advances, were now anxious to be included in the main operations against Japan.

The cycle of great international Anglo-American conferences concerned with the formulation of grand strategy came to an end at OCTAGON. The midwar era began with the tide turning against the Axis Powers and ended with the military situation under Allied control. It began when the Allies assumed the strategic initiative without having an agreed plan for the defeat of the primary foe, Germany. General Marshall's vigorous presentation of the American position for a concentrated cross-Channel attack in 1943, as opposed to the British contention for continued operations in the Mediterranean, marked the opening of the midwar era. In the beginning Great Britain was the senior partner, having greater war experience and many more divisions in the field. Its influence in the Western strategic councils was a dominating one. The U.S.S.R. was fighting for survival before the gates of Stalingrad and pleading for a second front.

But from Casablanca on, General Marshall and his U.S. staff had searched for an acceptable strategic formula against Germany that would ensure its speedy defeat and permit the United States to devote its efforts to the war with Japan. They hoped to perfect plans for the invasion and defeat in 1944—the primary objective of their strategic planning and debates of the midwar period. During the process the U.S. staff, which was intent on conducting a cross-Channel invasion, learned the art of compromise and to adjust its thinking to the two operations as its skill in military diplomacy grew.

By OCTAGON the strategy and plans against Germany, which had been hammered out during discussions, debates, and midwar conferences, and which embodied the American concept, were being fulfilled. The end of war with Germany looked very near in September 1944, but later events proved that the military planners were overoptimistic in their belief that the war would be over by the end of the year at the latest. The trend of the period was typified in the contrasting roles played by General Marshall at Casablanca and at OCTAGON. At Casablanca, as well as at TRIDENT,

QUADRANT, and SEXTANT, General Marshall had served as counsel for the American position. By OCTAGON, however, his midwar role as advocate was over. At that conference he appeared more as a principal architect of victory, advising and checking on the practically completed structure against the plans he had done so much to prepare.

During the Anglo-American strategic debates between Casablanca and OCTAGON, significant changes had taken place in the balance of military power within the coalition. These changes had as important implications for the determination of war strategy as for future relations among the partners in the wartime coalition. After Stalingrad the U.S.S.R. had steadily gathered strength and confidence and had made its weight felt in the strategic scales at the conferences at Moscow and Tehran. In the summer of 1944 the U.S.S.R. demonstrated by military successes during its advance across Europe that it was a power to be reckoned with by the West in the future political settlement of Europe. Further, by the close of the period the United States had begun to exceed the British in deployed military strength in the field in Europe.

OCTAGON was to be the last time in World War II that Churchill, proud guardian of British prestige and power, could boast that:

. . . the British Empire effort in Europe, counted in terms of divisions in the field, was about equal to that of the United States. This was as it should be. He was proud that the British Empire could claim equal partnership with their great ally, the United States, whom he regarded as the greatest military power in the world.

More significant for the future, however, was his admission that "the British Empire effort had now reached its peak, whereas that of their ally was ever increasing."

The Distribution of U.S. Military Might

At the end of almost three years of war General Marshall and his staff could regard the current state of the worldwide conflict with considerable satisfaction. Anglo-American differences had been few at OCTAGON, and coalition planning had reached its highest point. On the Continent, by the end of September 1944, Germany had been driven back to the doubtful safety of the West Wall, and France and Belgium had been largely cleared of the enemy. The

U.S.S.R. had moved into the Baltic provinces, occupying Estonia and the greater part of Latvia. Most of Bulgaria and Rumania in the Balkans were under Russian control, and the Germans were evacuating Greece. In the Pacific the Japanese high command watched with increasing uneasiness the American advance toward the strategic Formosa-Luzon–China Coast triangle. With the southern Palaus, Ulithi, and the Morotai under Allied control, the movement into the Philippines was not far distant. It was a cheerful moment for the strategic planners. The road ahead had never seemed freer of obstacles.

From a strategic viewpoint, the course of the war was now following the course originally laid out by the military planners. The main weight of the Army forces was being directed against the German war machine, which the planners estimated could not hold out much longer. Full attention could finally be given to the war in the Pacific, once Germany collapsed. The Army precept, "Knock Germany out first, then concentrate on Japan," gave indications of early fulfillment.

It had been a long struggle for General Marshall and his staff to assemble the American forces in the U.K. for the concentrated attack against Germany. The cream of the trained, equipped military manpower had been siphoned off during the first year after Pearl Harbor, and the available forces were deployed to fulfill the worldwide defensive and garrison requirements of that critical period. It was not until the latter part of 1942 that U.S. military power began to have any appreciable effect in the theaters of operations. The impact was not felt in northwest Europe, as the Army planners wanted, but in North Africa and at Guadalcanal.

During the second year, the period between Casablanca and SEXTANT, as the demands of diversionary offensive operations in the Pacific and Mediterranean increased, the Army staff gave serious consideration to the limitations on the supply of manpower. Further, it made strenuous efforts to conserve its growing military might for the cross-Channel invasion. Fewer U.S. divisions were sent overseas during that year of critical debate over global strategy than in 1942. Most of the year following the Casablanca Conference had passed before substantial U.S. ground combat power was being deployed to the U.K.

The deployment of U.S. Army forces from January through September was a continuation of the trend established in late 1943. Actually, in the first nine months of 1944, more divisions were sent overseas—the bulk going to the European theater—than had been shipped overseas during the previous two years. To support OVER-LORD and its follow-up operations, U.S. military forces were shipped to the ETO in ever increasing numbers during those nine months. At the end of the period, 34 divisions and 103 air groups (2,053,417 men) were in the European theater. That was more than 45 percent of the total number of troops overseas in all theaters. In the Mediterranean there were six divisions and 46 air groups (712,915 men). If the 9,354 troops stationed in Africa and the Middle East and the 27,739 assigned to the Persian Gulf Command were included, there would have been 40 divisions and 149 air groups (2,803,425 Army troops) concentrated on the defeat of Germany.

In the Pacific 21 divisions and 35 air groups (1,102,442 men) were deployed against Japan. Although no U.S. divisions were stationed in CBI, 149,014 troops manned the lines of communications, and 20 air groups operated from the theater. Despite reductions in the Alaskan garrison, 63,495 men, including two air groups, were on duty there at the end of September. Those far-flung forces totaled 1,314,931, including 21 Army divisions and 57 air groups, engaged in the war against Japan.

A comparison of the distribution of forces between the European and the Pacific–Far East wars indicates the concentration of forces against Germany that had begun in 1943. More than 75 percent of the 1,833,937 men shipped overseas during the first nine months of 1944 had been sent to the European area. Fewer than 25 percent had been assigned to the Pacific–Far East. The overall breakdown of Army troops overseas gave the war against Germany a two-to-one advantage over the Japanese conflict. The distribution of U.S. Army divisions was in the same ratio. Forty divisions were in Europe, 4 more were en route to the Mediterranean, and 21 were in the Pacific. The air strength was heavily in favor of Europe—149 groups or 72 percent as compared with 57 groups in the Pacific part of the world.

With the bulk of the Army's combat strength overseas deployed against the Reich, and with most of the divisions that were in the United States slated to go to the European theater, General Marshall and his planners could consider their original strategic concept well on the way to fulfillment. Although more than 3,500,000 men were still in the United States at the end of September, only 24 combat divisions remained. Most of these divisions were to be sent to Europe eventually, but the Army planners had hoped to maintain some of the divisions as a strategic reserve to cope with unforeseen emergencies. Estimates of the size of the reserve ranged from 5 to 15 divisions, but no official decision had been made by General Marshall. With Germany presumably on its last legs, there appeared little need to be concerned on that point. When the crisis caused by the breakthrough at Ardennes in December 1944 denuded the United States of all the remaining divisions, the strategic reserve became a memory. The possibility that too few divisions had been activated caused the War Department leaders, from Secretary Stimson down, some anxious moments. Secretary Stimson had never been happy about the 90-division gamble.

In addition to the 24 divisions, some 33 air groups were still assigned to the continental United States. They were mostly B-29 groups preparing for the Pacific war. But even were these groups to be sent to the Pacific, the greater part of the Army Air Forces would have been employed against Germany.

So, in the long run, General Marshall and his staff were not only able to reverse the trend toward the Pacific that had lasted well into 1943, but also went to the other extreme during 1944. As a result of unexpected developments in the European war, not one division was sent to the Pacific after August 1944, and planned deployment totals for the Pacific for 1944 were never attained. On the other hand, European deployment increased steadily and substantially exceeded the planners' estimates. By September 1944 it was evident that the Army was going to complete World War II according to the original strategic concept of "beat Germany first," and that the war against Japan would have to wait its turn. By the fall of 1944 the defeat of Hitler's Third Reich was certain. The only uncertainty was the exact timing.

Chapter IX

Strategic Survey of the War Against Germany and Japan

The War Against Germany

The increasing U.S. military power on the European continent was more than just a fulfillment of the original strategic concept of defeating Germany first. It was also the triumph of the U.S. staff principle of a decisive military war. To meet and defeat the German armies in combat was the goal toward which the Americans had been aiming. For that reason General Marshall and his staff had endeavored to prevent diversionary deployments in the midwar period. To reverse the 1942 trend and make the Mediterranean supply a strategic reserve for the cross-Channel operation had been part of the plan. The U.S. staff struggle from Casablanca onward— to limit the Mediterranean advances begun with TORCH, to prefer western over eastern Mediterranean operations, to reduce commitments to the Mediterranean, and to tie the Mediterranean undertakings to the support of the invasion of northwestern Europe— were all directed to the goal of concentrating the main American military might against the German military machine.

In 1943 that aim had taken concrete shape through General Marshall's efforts to ensure the return of seven U.S. and British divisions from the Mediterranean to the U.K. His efforts finally proved successful, much to the unhappiness of Prime Minister Churchill, who entertained high hopes for a more aggressive military policy in Italy and the eastern Mediterranean. In 1944 the struggle between the British and the Americans had largely revolved around General Marshall's efforts to remove more Allied combat forces from the Mediterranean in favor of the main continental drive, as opposed to Churchill's attempts to direct that strength toward the east. This time the debate centered around the southern France operation, endorsed by the U.S. staff, as opposed to Churchill's eastern Mediterranean and southeastern European policy. The American concept again won out.

The American staff's fear of a policy of attritional and peripheral warfare against Germany in the midwar years resulted from its continued anxiety over the ultimate costs in men, money, and time. That anxiety mounted with the growing realization of the ultimate limits of U.S. manpower. Although the staff was devoted to the principle of a decisive war, it was also fighting a war with a "guns-and-butter" policy. By 1943 the danger of overmobilization in the full tide of the war became apparent. If many more than ninety divisions were set aside as the nation's ground forces' "cutting edge," the guns-and-butter policy might have been seriously jeopardized. More Army divisions could have been activated, if necessary, to fight a war of attrition. That, however, would have cut into the production for U.S. and Allied forces, reduced the American standard of living for civilians and the military forces, and ultimately would have had adverse effects on domestic policies and on our relations with our Allies.

Neither the President nor the Army was eager to disturb the American economy or put an unnecessary hardship on the military and civilian population. The limits of available military manpower and the fear of the effects of a long drawn-out period of maximum mobilization confirmed the Army's concept of defeating Germany by a direct concentrated effort with a minimum of time, money, and manpower. By OCTAGON the U.S. concept of a decisive strategy was the basis of the Allied strategic decisions that were in the process of being realized.

The increase of American military might over the British confirmed a trend that had begun to appear at SEXTANT. By the end of 1943 the Americans had finally managed to reverse the trend of the first year and a half after Pearl Harbor, during which the concepts of the more highly mobilized and experienced British had largely prevailed in the Western Allied strategy councils. At the close of 1943 the Americans, backed by their mighty industrial and military establishments operating at full steam, had, with Soviet assistance, made the British yield to their ideas of continental strategy. The growing disparity between British military strength and that of the United States and the Soviets began to show up more clearly after the summer of 1944. When the war against Germany continued beyond the hoped-for end in 1944, British influence in the Allied councils declined further.

Between the increasing strength of the U.S. forces driving eastward to destroy the German armies, and the forces of the U.S.S.R. that were advancing into central and southeastern Europe, the British were left to salvage what they could of their European and Mediterranean policies. The Allies entered the last year of the war with the foundations of the coalition in further transition: British influence was on the wane, and the United States and the U.S.S.R. were emerging as the two strongest military powers in Europe. Churchill was aware of the American determination to withdraw from the Continent as quickly as possible after the defeat of Germany, and with the increasing signs of Soviet entrenchment in central and southeastern Europe, he became alarmed.

In view of the growing political character of the coalition war, Churchill could not understand the singleness of purpose of the Washington authorities bent solely on the speedy destruction of German military power. Later, in his book, *Triumph and Tragedy,* he wrote: "In Washington especially longer and wider views should have prevailed." Although the Prime Minister and the U.S. staff did not agree on the importance of military versus political objectives in the concluding phases of the European war, Churchill was not alone in his awareness that the defeat of Germany might leave the Soviet Union the dominant power on the European Continent. In the summer of 1944 the U.S. military staff advised the Secretary of State:

> While the war with Germany is well advanced towards final conclusion, the defeat of Germany will leave Russia in a position of assured military dominance in eastern Europe and in the Middle East. While it is true the U.S. and British will occupy and control western Europe, their strength in that area will thereafter progressively decline with the withdrawal of all but their occupational and enforcement forces, for employment against Japan, or for demobilization.

The U.S. military staff also foresaw the inevitable emergence of the U.S.S.R. as the dominant power on the continent of Asia as well as Europe:

> In estimating Russia's probable course as regards Japan, we

must balance against such assurances as we have received from
Russia, the fact that whether or not she enters the war, the fall
of Japan will leave Russia in a dominant position on continental
Northeast Asia, and, in so far as military power is concerned,
able to impose her will in all that region.

The staff also observed that the great historic changes in the international military balance in process would have important reper-
cussions on the international political situation:

> The successful termination of the war against our present
> enemies will find a world profoundly changed in respect of rela-
> tive national military strengths, a change more comparable in-
> deed with that occasioned by the fall of Rome than with any
> other change occurring during the succeeding fifteen hundred
> years. This is a fact of fundamental importance in its bearing
> upon future international political settlements and all discus-
> sions leading thereto. Aside from the elimination of Germany
> and Japan as military powers, and developments in the relative
> economic power of principal nations, there are technical and
> material factors which have contributed greatly to this change.
> Among these are the development of aviation, the general
> mechanization of warfare, and the marked shift in the munition-
> ing potentials of the great powers.
>
> After the defeat of Japan, the United States and the Soviet
> Union will be the only military powers of the first magnitude.
> This is due in each case to a combination of geographical po-
> sition and extent, and vast munitioning potential. While the
> U.S. can project its military power into many areas overseas,
> it is nevertheless true that the relative strength and geographic
> positions of these two powers preclude the military defeat of
> one of these powers by the other, even if that power were allied
> with the British Empire . . .

The memorandum, which was prepared by the JSSC and forwarded
by the JCS on Aug. 3, 1944, also commented on the British position
after the war:

> Both in an absolute and relative sense . . . the British Em-
> pire will emerge from the war having lost ground both eco-
> nomically and militarily.

Being aware of growing and possibly irreconcilable conflicts between their partners in the coalition that might impede the progress of the war, the U.S. staff advocated postponement of territorial settlements until the military phase of the global conflict was concluded. Receiving no instructions to the contrary, the military staff devoted its attention to employing the resources and manpower in the war against Germany to end that conflict as quickly as possible. By the summer of 1944 the U.S. armed forces was a highly proficient fighting machine and, in conjunction with the British, functioned with great precision. The military staff would win the decisive military victory it had set out to achieve, and it would leave to the heads of government and their political advisers the problems of territorial and political settlements. Thus for the American military planners, the war against Germany was to be concluded as they had wished to wage it from the beginning—a conventional war of mass concentration.

The War Against Japan

One of the primary reasons behind the goal of bringing the war against Germany to an end as quickly as possible was the desire to ensure the defeat of Japan as quickly and cheaply as possible. Concern over the Pacific war caused the military staff to intensify its efforts in the midwar period to reach a final settlement with the British on European strategy. In Europe, the United States, despite its growing military power, shared equal responsibility with the British for strategy. In the war against Japan, however, the United States, by virtue of its location, resources, and manpower, had been the predominant partner from the beginning.

General Marshall and his staff had determined that the two wars were to be waged as distinct but related efforts. The war in Europe had finally been settled by OCTAGON into the type of warfare sought by the Army planners. The war against Japan, fought across a vast ocean, in the air, in jungles, on islands, and on the sea, promised to follow more unconventional lines. Although the exact timing, complete resources, and the final shape of Allied contributions to the defeat of Japan still depended on the end of the European war, American forces advanced so rapidly across the Pacific that by the summer of 1944 they were exceeding their most accelerated schedules. But before Japan was finally encircled, the American planners were destined to learn more about the costs of waging a "secondary" and "limited" war in the Pacific—a war that would not stand still.

Aside from the final shaping of European strategy, the outstanding feature of the midwar period for the Army planners was the evolution of the Pacific war into a dynamic movement that generated its own operations and compelled greater and greater attention to offensive strategy. After the Guadalcanal campaign had been launched and the strategic initiative seized, the Americans felt that they had no choice but to go on with the advance. Each forward step demanded another. As the Japanese outposts were beaten back, the approach to the larger well-defended land masses presented increased demands for men, planes, and shipping. Often these demands were in excess of the personnel and resources the Army was willing to allocate to the secondary war.

During 1942 and early 1943 decisions had usually been made in favor of larger increments of troops and resources for the Pacific. That was easily understood, because the Japanese had to be contained, and no definite plans for the defeat of Europe had been agreed upon. The balancing of "diversions" to the Mediterranean by parallel allocations to the Pacific continued through 1943. If the Mediterranean threatened to become, in General Marshall's phrase, "a suction pump," the Pacific became, in a sense, the American safety valve.

General Marshall and his staff never forgot that Germany was to be defeated first and while at the Pacific Military Conference in March 1943 they had endeavored to curb the Pacific expansion. They realized that if the increasing requirements of the Pacific were not checked, the means for defeating Germany by a cross-Channel invasion might find its way into the war against Japan. The Army, therefore, became less generous with its resources. It was a difficult task for General Marshall and his military staff because they had to contend with the persistent demands of Army commanders in the secondary war, increasing pressure from the Navy to speed up the war and make full use of the fast-growing Pacific Fleet, and the efforts of the British and Chinese to obtain U.S. ground troops for CBI.

Both Generals MacArthur and Stilwell were anxious to proceed with their campaigns. Their requests for more resources and troops were a symptom of a general condition that the Army planners referred to as "localitis." Unfortunately, it was almost impossible to change. Their requests were handled sympathetically by the Army planners, who endeavored to find a way of meeting at least part of the requirements if it could be done without upsetting European plans.

Dealing with the Navy, however, was a somewhat more complex

problem. In trying to maintain harmonious relations among the sister services as well as with the Allies, General Marshall probably felt as if he were engaged in a double coalition war in the Pacific. The main portion of the Navy's strength was in the Pacific Fleet, and the Navy was eager to push the campaign across the Pacific with all its potential. The fact that the Army's chief interest was in the opposite direction—in Europe—and that General Marshall permitted Admiral King to be the spokesman for the U.S. role in the Pacific during CCS meetings, frequently led to complications. The difficulties arose mainly from the inability of the Army and Navy to agree upon an overall commander for the Pacific rather than from a lack of agreement on the correct route to Japan. Although the Army recognized the growing strength and primary interest of the Navy in the Pacific, it still did not feel it could relinquish its position as co-equal in the Pacific as long as General MacArthur commanded the bulk of the Army forces there. General Marshall appreciated the advantages of opening a new front against Japan in the Central Pacific, but he faithfully defended General MacArthur's views in the JCS meetings and was able to maintain the New Guinea–Philippines approach in spite of the opinion of many joint planners that the Central Pacific should be the main route. Had the command problem been resolved, the JCS preoccupation with the continuing problems of routes and resources could have been minimized and the latter problems left largely to the discretion of the overall commander. But with the Army backing General MacArthur and the Navy backing Admiral Nimitz, agreement proved impossible, and interservice negotiation and compromise provided the only solution.

The Army had a different problem in the Far East. Whereas the Army was constantly urging action and expanded operations, the British and Chinese were largely content to hold onto what they had in Burma and China. So instead of playing a restraining role the Army staff pressed constantly for forward movement, and gave what support it could to General Stilwell in his endeavors to spur the British and Chinese to greater efforts. While engaging in this usually unrewarding activity, the Army at the same time had to ward off requests from those two allies for more U.S. planes, equipment, and personnel. To get the British and Chinese to commit their forces to a campaign in CBI and simultaneously prevent the involvement of additional U.S. resources, especially the ground forces, was often a feat more befitting a tightrope walker than a professional soldier.

It required a great deal of ingenuity and fortitude to hold out against those influential countries, but General Marshall played the role of the mediator and succeeded in hoarding the bulk of the Army divisions and manpower for OVERLORD. He encouraged full naval and air action in the Pacific, which allowed the Navy to expend its surplus energy while he retained control of the limited supply of U.S. divisions. In CBI he urged complete employment of British, Indian, and Chinese ground forces supported by Army Air Forces units and service troops rather than U.S. combat divisions, by either evading or denying requests from the Prime Minister, the General-issimo, and General Stilwell for U.S. divisions.

It had been especially difficult to resist the attempts to build up Army commitments in the war against Japan before the decision at SEXTANT to mount OVERLORD. But with the definite agreement on European operations, the task became considerably easier. First priority went to OVERLORD, which served to slow down Pacific deployment. In the midwar era Pacific deployments fell into the pre-SEXTANT period when Mediterranean commitments permitted the Pacific effort to expand concomitantly, and the more stringent post-SEXTANT period, when the requirements for OVERLORD had a first call on Army resources and the excessive growth in the Pacific was definitely slowed down.

The slowdown was not intended to signify that the Army wished to prevent the full prosecution of the war against Japan while the conflict against Germany was still in progress. It did mean that the Army realized the necessity for fighting Japan with the forces and resources available, rather than with those desirable. The long-range planning that reached its peak during the latter months of 1943 was an expression of the desire of the Army planners to limit the Army effort in the Pacific until the European war was settled. When General Marshall put an end to long-range planning just prior to SEXTANT and endorsed a policy of flexibility or opportunism, it looked as if the constant drain caused by hit-or-miss operations would continue. However, the OVERLORD commitment, which followed almost immediately, placed a more effective block on Pacific expansion than perhaps the adoption of a definitely scheduled long-range plan might have provided.

The succession of shipping and landing craft shortages and imbalances exerted a direct influence on both the deployment and operational activities in the Pacific. The long line of communications and the need for a great deal of shipping as well as service personnel to operate the far end of the line effectively also acted as a controlling factor. As long as shipping was in short supply, the Pacific buildup could not proceed indiscriminately.

Even though the Army staff in Washington attempted to hold down the buildup of forces in the Pacific, General Marshall was a firm believer in making the best use of what he had. He was constantly seeking a better and quicker way of ending the war, and he encouraged the employment of America's superior air and naval weapons and the introduction of more effective instruments of warfare.

Although conducting a dynamic war on a flexible basis permitted a wide range of operational choices, as far as the Army staff was concerned military need was the controlling factor during 1943–44. The Army welcomed all Allies who could contribute to the defeat of Japan, shorten the length of the war, and perhaps reduce the number of casualties that the United States would have to suffer. At the same time it consistently refrained from becoming involved in matters pertaining to their former colonial territories. General Marshall and his staff favored the use of British, French, and Chinese troops in CBI and Dutch forces in the SWPA on the ground that those nations could best cope with their overrun possessions either singly or in concert. They also favored entry of the U.S.S.R. into the war to engage the Japanese armies in northern China and Korea and to relieve any future American invasion of Japan of threats from this area.

The Army intended neither to interfere with operations to reinvest former colonial areas, nor to assist the forces of the U.S. Allies in the task of resubjugation unless the military requirements for such undertakings could be closely related to the defeat of Japan. The objective was to bring the war to a quick conclusion and to save American lives without becoming involved in political and economic problems in the Far East. At the same time, the Army staff realized that the Allies were determined to conduct operations to repossess their overrun colonial territories. Anticipating such a drive in the SEAC–Netherlands East Indies area, the Army planners felt that operations against the northern and eastern coasts of Borneo, though not essential to the defeat of Japan, would militarily be the most rewarding tasks that could be undertaken in that area. The operations would provide control over the South China Sea, Java Sea, Sunda Strait, and Makassar Strait exits and would not interfere unduly with the main effort to the north.

During 1944 the emergence of political consciousness among the Army staff was increasingly noticeable, and gave every indication of becoming even more significant in the future. As the conflict came closer to the Japanese homeland, questions of political significance began to arise. From a military viewpoint, General Marshall looked approvingly on the British wish to participate in the main operations against Japan. Both he and his staff realized the political motivation behind their desire. The Army and the Navy agreed on keeping the Central Pacific an American preserve, and the Chief of Staff was content to let Admiral King argue the question of a British fleet under Admiral Nimitz. Introduction of a third party into a determination of Pacific operational strategy might have made the situation so complex as to require that decisions be made on a higher level. Being well acquainted with the Prime Minister's concepts of strategy for the war against Japan, neither General Marshall nor Admiral King would have wanted that.

Nevertheless, increasing British insistence on a full share in the war against Japan, especially in naval and air operations, led to an extension of General Marshall's intermediary position in the Pacific war among the Navy, the Army Air Forces, and General MacArthur. The Navy was anxious to reap the prestige to which it felt its exploits entitled it, and the AAF, anxious to complete its war record in a blaze of glory, considered the British offer of aid friendly but competitive. With the Army's prestige less directly involved, General Marshall's role became even more important.

Growing political problems presented matters beyond the competence of the military staff to resolve without more guidance from the President, but as 1944 wore on, his deteriorating physical condition became more apparent. His illnesses became more frequent, and he needed longer periods of recuperation. As the need for his guidance and political skill increased, his ability to provide it decreased. There was no certainty that the Army staff would be prepared to cope with the political problems as well as it had the military questions in the absence of political direction. The lifetime of the military staff members had been devoted to determining the most efficient, expeditious method of defeating an enemy, but the complexities of diplomatic maneuvering, national political problems, and political and economic negotiations were areas in which most of the staff had had little previous experience.

The China problem was the most difficult for the Army staff. There the diverse and complicated elements, both native and foreign, were combined in a veritable maze. China's struggle against Japan had won popular sympathy in the United States and, although little accurate information was available on conditions in China, Americans had a feeling of helping an underdog in an uneven conflict. The Army was abundantly aware of the unhappy state of the Chinese armies, and it had entertained hopes that Chinese manpower could be trained and equipped to fight the Japanese and that air bases could be built in China to strike at the Japanese homeland. The Army made determined efforts to get supplies and airpower to China during the first two years of the war. The airlift was expanded, the line of communications was improved, roads were constructed, and pipelines were laid to help China. U.S. officers and military equipment were sent to CBI in an effort to make the Chinese Nationalist armies into modern fighting organizations. The Chinese economy was supported by generous Federal aid. Those stop-gap measures were utilized to keep China in the war until land and sea approaches could again be opened.

One of the most important factors in the Chinese puzzle was the attitude of President Roosevelt and his political advisers. They, too, hoped to see China grow strong and democratic and become a stabilizing power in the Far East, but, vacillating between the hopes and realities of the conditions in China, they followed tactics toward achieving their hopes that were not consistent. With the public sympathy over China's past, the Army concerned with China's present, and the President visualizing its future, the overall picture was seen from varying points of view.

With the U.S. Army staff engaged in fighting a decisive military war against Japan, the Chinese aversion to engaging the enemy decisively was disillusioning. Chiang Kai-shek's concern over the Chinese Communists, and the conditions he laid down on committing his troops against the Japanese, deflated the Army's hopes that Chinese manpower would play an effective role in the war. However, the use of Chinese air forces remained a possibility until the Japanese thrust into the Kweilin area in mid-1944. The loss of those airfields and the prospect of operating B-29's from bases in the Marianas ended the Army's hopes for effective air support from Chinese bases in the war against Japan. As a consequence China's military importance in the war rapidly depreciated. Nevertheless, American commitments to China continued, and the Army accepted the task of supporting China as a necessary though limited burden.

While that change was in progress, General Marshall and the Army staff had consistently supported General Stilwell's efforts to obtain Chinese cooperation. The Army, however, was only one element in the complex situation, and it had to cope with the Stilwell-Chennault controversy as well as with British, Chinese, and American pressures. Furthermore, China was only one part, and a relatively minor one, in the worldwide strategic picture with which the Army was concerned. The removal of General Stilwell in October 1944 provided some relief for the situation and paved the way for a more impersonal approach to China's role in the war. However, with little consistent political guidance from the President, and with U.S. postwar objectives in the Far East largely idealistic, and the methods of achieving them still undetermined, the Army's task of preparing China's forces for the challenges that lay ahead were enormous.

Aside from the China problem, the military situation looked very favorable to General Marshall and his staff by October 1944. In the Pacific the Japanese were confused, uncertain, and forced to rely more than ever on their ground forces. The Japanese Air Force had already been reduced to a second-rate power; and though the Japanese Navy still had powerful battle units, it was unwilling to risk them in an engagement unless key points in the Empire's defense system were threatened. The Allies now had the advantages of surprise and superior air and naval forces. The Allies could select the time and place, and force the Japanese to fight on Allied terms. That was a complete reversal of the 1942 period when the Japanese had held the initiative.

The Army staff was confident that adequate air and naval power would be on hand to carry out the assigned operations in the Pacific, although the service troop shortage might slow the advance unless Germany was defeated quickly. Ground forces appeared to be adequate for a Philippines campaign, and by the time that was completed, additional U.S. combat divisions should become available from Europe. There might be some local squeezes on shipping, but shipping in the Pacific was adequate to meet the expected requests. Although manpower and supplies might be a little tight on occasions, there appeared to be sufficient forces and supplies to recapture the Philippines.

In the final phases of the debate over Luzon and Formosa, those were the controlling factors. The JCS decision during OCTAGON to advance the target date of the attack on Leyte to Oct. 20 had permitted the planning date for Luzon to be advanced to Dec. 20. The means to undertake the Formosa operation were still unavailable since the war against Germany was still in progress and showed no signs of ending in the near future. On Oct. 3, after two weeks of debate, the JCS decided that General MacArthur should take Luzon after Leyte. Admiral Nimitz would support General MacArthur during the operations in the Philippines and then would occupy positions in the Bonin Islands in January 1945 and in the Ryukyus in

March. The operations ultimately made the seizure of Formosa unnecessary.

Military planning in the war against Japan entered its last stages in the fall of 1944. Plans were being prepared to redeploy troops and equipment considered necessary to conclude the war against Japan as soon as they could be spared from the struggle in Europe. Tentative dates for the end of the European war were established, and shipping schedules were drawn up. As soon as Germany surrendered, the stream of men and supplies would begin to flow to the Pacific.

The Strategic Bombing Survey

In view of the high cost and heavy share of the war effort that was associated with strategic bombing, the AAF laid plans to measure the potentialities of airpower against actual achievements even before the war was over. Toward the end of March 1944, proposals were formulated to survey the effects of the bomber offensive on Germany when it was available for an autopsy. But what started out as a purely AAF effort was expanded to include Army and Navy members and, instead of reporting to the Chief of AAF, the new organization would report to the Secretary of War and the President. The AAF evaluation boards that were sent to each theater were made responsible for studying tactical bombings.

On Sept. 9, 1944, President Roosevelt signed the directive establishing the U.S. Strategic Bombing Survey (USSBS), and a few weeks later the USSBS opened its headquarters at 20 Grosvenor Square, London. During the fall and winter of 1944–45, the organization was built up to its authorized strength of 350 officers, 350 civilians, and 500 enlisted men, and the personnel were trained for conducting the survey. In April 1945 trained teams moved into Germany to obtain government and business records and seek out German prisoners who might be helpful in reconstructing the bomber offensive as experienced by the Germans. Following V-E (Victory in Europe) Day, specialized groups operated out of an advance headquarters in Frankfurt for about ninety days, gathering data and statistics, interviewing thousands of former German officers and civilians of all categories, and inspecting the ruins of many plants, factories, and cities. Despite promises made at the Yalta Conference (Feb. 3–11, 1945), survey teams were not permitted to enter the Russian zones of Germany. By the fall of 1945, most of the USSBS had returned to Washington, where more than 200 reports were prepared and submitted to the Secretary of War. An excellent study—"The Contribution of Air

Power to the Defeat of Germany"—had also been made by an AAF headquarters in Europe, but the USSBS reports were accepted as conclusive findings on the effects of strategic bombing.

The achievements and the errors of some of the target systems of the strategic bombing campaign were clearly pointed out in the USSBS. The gaining and maintaining of air supremacy by the Allied air forces was the most significant of all achievements because it enabled the bomber forces to destroy the German aircraft industry. During 1943 and the early months of 1944, Allied bomber losses were heavy, but commencing in the spring of 1944, probable bomber losses did not deter attacks on strategic targets as they had earlier. In the spring of 1944, 75 percent of the Reich's aircraft industry was destroyed or heavily damaged; but the USSBS confirmed the judgments of qualified Germans who reported that aircraft engine factories would have been better targets for the bombing offensive than the aircraft assembly plants.

The Allied bombing offensive against Germany's ball-bearing industry was a phase of the campaign against aircraft production. Attacks on the few concentrated factories in August 1943, made without long-range fighter escort, were extremely costly to the Allies in men and planes and, though good results were achieved, the destruction was not complete. Air attacks were resumed the following spring, but, in the meantime, production of the ball-bearing industry had fallen 40 to 50 percent as a result of the dispersal of the factories. The USSBS reported that although German armament production was not materially affected by a shortage of bearings, many tank commanders charged the high level of tank unserviceability to defective bearings.

The German oil production industry had a top priority in the bombing effort. Although Germany had adequate supplies of crude oil and was increasing production of synthetic oil in April 1944, one year later the supplies were virtually nonexistent, and production had been reduced to about 5 percent of the former output. The USSBS pointed out that German oil, chemical, and rubber industries were closely related, and that attacks conducted earlier in the war against ethyl-, methanol-, and nitrogen-producing plants would probably have been more decisive. The USSBS also considered that there should have been less blind bombing of industrial areas and more selective bombing in the campaign against oil production. Nevertheless, the report concluded that the Allied bombing effort effectively stopped oil production with decisive military consequences.

Another target system of high priority was the German transportation network. Germany had one of the finest railway systems in the world when the war began. Although the air offensive was planned to halt the movement of troops and all categories of supplies and equipment for war, it had an even greater effect on the economy of the country. By the spring of 1945, only railway traffic of the highest military priority was able to move and no shipments of food were made, even to stricken cities. The decline in the capacity of carloadings and marshaling yards in the main industrial areas of Germany was catastrophic. The main north German canals were blocked; Rhine River traffic was interdicted; the Danube was mined; and the Allied tactical air forces joined in the campaign by bombing bridges and tunnels and shooting up key railside installations. The USSBS commented that if the bombing campaign had been initiated earlier, the French and Belgian transportation systems might have been saved. The report concluded, however, that the air offensive on transportation was the decisive blow that completely disorganized the German economy.

German tank and truck production and ordnance depots were also included in the strategic bombing offensive. That campaign was undertaken because the German forces had lost so much equipment in Poland and France that a large-scale reequipping program was essential for homeland defense. Prior to August 1944 those targets were bombed only occasionally, but in the fall of 1944 assembly plants and ordnance depots frequently had second priority in the strategic offensive. After examining what remained of several plants, the USSBS concluded that possibly 64 percent of the tank plants and an even greater percentage of truck plants had been destroyed. Estimates indicated that 2,250 tanks, assault guns, and self-propelled guns, and 40 percent of the motor vehicles destined for German army units were never delivered.

Three other German target systems—steel production, submarine assembly, and V-weapons—were included in the strategic bombing offensive. The steel plants suffered a 25 percent loss in production, and their plans for expansion were halted by Allied air strikes. The air attacks on the submarine industry were more successful. More than 100,000 tons of bombs were dropped on installations that contributed to the U-boat warfare. As a result, Germany's production of submarines was seriously delayed. Of the 423 large, fast Type 21 and Type 23 submarines that were planned, only 180 were built. Concerning the Allied air offensive against the original V-weapon launching sites along the French coast, the USSBS concluded that the bombing probably delayed the beginning of the "buzz-bomb" launchings against England by three or four months.

The USSBS also confirmed the reports of German authorities that German electric power stations had been highly vulnerable to air attack. American air objective planners apparently believed that either the system was more highly developed than it actually was, and therefore less vulnerable, or that it would be destroyed as a side effect of the many strikes against the industrial cities of Germany. In any case, the electric power industry was never selected as a primary bombing objective.

The final report of the USSBS affirmed that the victory in the air was complete, and that Allied airpower had been decisive in the war in Western Europe. Its overall conclusion was as follows:

> Allied air power was decisive in the war in western Europe. Hindsight inevitably suggests that it might have been employed differently or better in some respects. Nevertheless, it was decisive. In the air, its victory was complete; at sea, its contribution, combined with naval power, brought an end to the enemy's greatest naval threat—the U-boat; on land, it helped turn the tide overwhelmingly in favor of Allied ground forces. Its power and superiority made possible the success of the invasion. It brought the economy which sustained the enemy's armed forces to virtual collapse, although the full effects of this collapse had not reached the enemy's front lines when they were overrun by Allied forces. It brought home to the German people the full impact of modern war with all its horror and suffering. Its imprint on the German nation will be lasting.

On Aug. 15, 1945, President Harry S. Truman requested the USSBS to make a comparatively broad survey of the air war against Japan. A further directive to study the effects of all types of air attack in the war against Japan expanded the scope of the survey. Tactical and strategic operations were to be considered, and the employment of the naval air arm, as well as the AAF, was to be included. Teams of experts who had acquired valuable experience in the assessment of pertinent evidence in Germany surveyed the ruins of Japanese cities and factories, gathered production statistics, conducted medical and psychological studies, and reviewed Japanese defensive actions.

The relationship between the B-29 bombing attacks against various Japanese war industries and the loss of production in each is shown in the statistics compiled by the USSBS for the period from the peak production month in 1944 to July 1945. The consumption of coal and electric power, conventional indexes of industrial output, fell about 50 percent—although the coal industry was not bombed, and electric power-generating stations were only incidentally damaged during urban raids. Air-frame factories lost 60 percent of their plant capacity, and production dropped to 40 percent; aircraft engine factories lost 75 percent of their capacity, and their production fell to 25 percent. In the oil-refining field, 83 percent of the capacity was destroyed, and production fell to about 15 percent; however, part of the cause for the low production was the fact that the oil supplies were already depleted, and the refineries were operating at a low rate. Shipyards, which had a 15 percent capacity loss, had a production loss of about 75 percent, but a steel shortage was a contributing cause to the drop. At the same time, the output from the small radio and radio parts factories, upon which the electronic industry depended, was drastically reduced by area bombing attacks.

The USSBS made a study of industry in thirty-nine representative Japanese cities, and it estimated that in plants damaged by bombing, production had fallen to 27 percent of the peak by July 1945. In undamaged plants, the production had fallen to 54 percent; and in all plants, damaged or undamaged, it had fallen to 35 percent. The figures suggested that strategic bombardment had less effect on production in Japanese industry as a whole than the shortages caused by the blockade.

Airpower, however, played an extremely important role in the blockade and, according to USSBS estimates accounted for 40 percent of all shipping sunk. Mines planted by B-29's in a short, five-month campaign sank 9.3 percent of all merchant tonnage lost during the war. The USSBS suggested that the XX Bomber Command might have been more profitably employed against shipping and oil targets than in strikes against naval dockyards and arsenals, engine and aircraft factories, and steel mills in Japan, and several targets on Formosa from its China bases; and that the XXI Bomber Command should have put more effort toward exploiting difficulties caused by earlier attacks on shipping. That would have meant stepping up B-29 mine-planting operations and an air offensive against Japan's railway transportation system. The system was already overloaded and vulnerable to attack. Following that reasoning, a carrier attack on the Hakodate-Amori ferry in August 1944— instead of July 1945—plus B-29 attacks on the Kammon Tunnel and certain easily obstructed points on the railway would have cut off all coal shipments and strangled Japan's economy.

Various Japanese leaders attributed the decline in factory production to the B-29 bombing effort. In nine months, B-29 raids caused 806,000 civilian casualties, of whom 330,000 were killed. Pre-raid evacuation and post-raid mass migration displaced an estimated 8,500,000 people. During the fire raids and atomic bomb attacks, the air raid protection facilities were hopelessly inadequate. The blockade caused a serious food shortage, and undernourishment brought disease and lowered morale and efficiency. Factory output was bound to suffer. By the end of the war the B-29's had dropped about 145,000 tons of bombs on Japan and had destroyed about 40 percent of the built-up areas in sixty-six cities. About 105 square miles in the centers of Japan's six most important industrial cities were devastated.

The war in the Pacific was basically a struggle for mastery of the air over the seas. The USSBS states: "Control of the air was essential to the success of every major military operation, . . ." but it had been the "coordinated teamplay of the ground, sea and air forces, both ground-based and carrier-based, and their supporting services, backed up by the full effort of all phases of the home front that enabled us to secure control of the air, at first locally and then more generally, culminating in virtual freedom of the skies over the Japanese home islands themselves."

Although the USSBS properly refrained from giving any single service principal credit for winning the war, Japanese leaders were not reluctant to comment, and many of them attributed primary importance to airpower in general, others specifically to the bombing of the home islands. Prince Fumimaro Konoye stated: "Fundamentally the thing that brought about the determination to make peace was the prolonged bombing by the B-29's."

Chapter X

Epilogue

Strategic military planning for the coalition World War II, with the exception of how to defeat Japan, came to an end in late 1944. After the Allied forces had become firmly established on the European continent and had begun the pursuit of the German forces, the Supreme Allied Commander was responsible for making tactical decisions as the requirements of the situation dictated. For General Marshall and his staff it was mainly a matter of logistics. But as Prime Minister Churchill watched the swiftly advancing Russian forces move into Poland and the Balkans, the war became a great political contest for important stakes. He wanted Western Allied forces diverted to the areas vacated by the retreating Germans in southeastern Europe to forestall a Soviet purge. The final year of the war against Germany was fundamentally a question of military tactics vis-à-vis political maneuvers.

If President Roosevelt had joined with the Prime Minister, as he often had, the U.S. military staff's concentration on bringing the war against Germany to a swift and decisive victory might have been slowed down and the war directed into political areas. However, the President would not, and, by himself, the Prime Minister could not. Possibly the reason the President would not was because when political objectives conflicted with the possibility of a quick military victory, he usually chose the latter. Also, becoming more exhausted with the burden he was carrying, he was perhaps anxious to conclude the war and apply his failing strength to the problems of peace. The President's health had begun to fail after SEXTANT, and his absences from Washington top-level council meetings had become more frequent. In any event the President was caught in the middle of a political dilemma in the coalition war by 1944–45. It is not believed that the President was insensitive or unconcerned about the unilateral efforts of the U.S.S.R. to influence the shape of postwar Europe. From a domestic political consideration he had to wage a speedy, decisive war that justified the entry of the United States and the shipment of U.S. troops overseas. He had educated the American public to the need for active participation, but whether he could have led them through the prolonged war or an extended period of occupational duty by U.S. troops—which might have resulted from the more active American role in southeastern Europe urged by Churchill—was somewhat doubtful.

The American tradition of remaining aloof from European affairs, the spirit of isolationism quieted temporarily by the global war, and the typical aversion of a democratic nation to extended war efforts would undoubtedly have made him less inclined in 1944–45 to risk new military or political involvements on the Continent in the process of ending the conflict. The experience of World War I and domestic political realism appeared to prescribe that a President of the United States who led his country in international war must stay in only long enough to defeat the enemy decisively, hasten out of the war, disarrange the American standard of living and way of life as little as possible, get the troops home, and return to the traditional policy of avoiding involvement in European affairs.

As envisaged by President Roosevelt, the European path of peace appeared to be one of long-range development of a healthy environment in which new moral, political, and economic factors might come into action instead of the traditional balance of military and political power. Certain actions, other than placing U.S. forces in the path of the Soviet advance, had occurred to him as feasible ways of keeping the peace in Europe with friends and foes alike. It is purely academic whether in time these would have amounted to an effective working policy, or would have remained what they were in the summer of 1944—a number of incipient threads, a composite of idealism and practicality, of optimism and reality.

The President appeared to have put his faith in offering the U.S.S.R. the hand of friendship; in his personal handling of Premier Stalin and the Premier's reasonableness; in a joint occupation of Europe with a million-man U.S. force to remain in certain selected areas of Germany for one or two years; in raising the economic standards of relatively backward areas and thereby preventing trouble spots from developing, as in Iran; in the new international establishment, the United Nations Organization; and in a system of United Nations' trusteeships over key bases, as in North Africa. Nevertheless, in the final year of the war, American national policy placed no obstacles in the path of concluding the European war by a decisive military victory.

By the summer of 1944 old problems that had been dormant and new problems arising from Allied operations on the Continent became very much in evidence and required immediate attention. These problems called for policy decisions relating to Allied, liberated, and neutral countries. General Eisenhower was given more and more responsibility for political decisions, or else fell heir to them by default. His decisions were made on the basis of military considerations, since he received no clear political guidance or instructions from Washington. In so doing, General Eisenhower used the American military staff concept of ending the war quickly and decisively with the least number of casualties. That trend became even more apparent in 1945 when he decided to stop at the Elbe River and not take Berlin or Prague ahead of the Russians.

General Marshall and the U.S. staff consistently backed up General Eisenhower's decisions. Two statements prepared by General Marshall in April 1945 reflected his usual approach. One was in response to the British proposal to capture Berlin. The other concerned the liberation of Prague and western Czechoslovakia. With reference to Berlin, the JCS members agreed with General Marshall's statement to the British Chiefs of Staff, ". . . that the destruction of the German armed forces is more important than any political or psychological advantages which might be derived from possible capture of the German capital ahead of the Russians. . . . Only Eisenhower is in a position to make a decision concerning his battle and the best way to exploit successes to the full." With respect to Prague and the rest of Czechoslovakia, General Marshall commented in a message to General Eisenhower: "Personally and aside from all logistic, tactical or strategical implications, I would be loath to hazard American lives for purely political purposes. Czechoslovakia will have to be cleared of German troops and we may have to cooperate with the Russians in so doing."

Those views of the Army Chief of Staff took on additional significance because during the interruption between President Roosevelt's final days in office and his successor's early days, the burden of deciding important issues fell heavily on the senior military advisers in Washington. General Marshall's position on the issues presented were always in accord with the Army's earlier strategic planning concepts. Whatever the ultimate political implications, from the point of view of a decisive military ending of the war against Germany it made little difference whether the forces of the United States or those of the U.S.S.R. took Berlin or Prague.

Churchill's inability to reverse the trend of the last year of the war was indicative of the changed relationship between the American and British national military power and of the changing bases within the Allied coalition. The military power assembled by General Marshall for the invasion of Europe was a tremendous weapon, but the United States refrained from using it for political purposes. The Prime Minister possessed the purpose but he lacked the power. British mobilization was practically complete by the end of 1943, but with its manpower fully mobilized, stresses and strains began to appear in its economy during the first half of 1944.

British production became increasingly unbalanced after the middle of 1944, and the British fought the rest of the war with a contracting economy. Having entered the war later than the British, the Americans enjoyed the advantages of greater industrial capacity and manpower resources. The United States reached the peak of its military manpower mobilization in May 1945, the month Germany surrendered. Reaching its war production peak at the end of 1943, the United States was able to sustain it at a high level, keep it balanced with nonwar production, taper off somewhat in 1944, and still more in 1945 to V-E Day.

During the last year of the European war the greater capacity of the American economy and population to support a sustained, large-scale Allied offensive effort was clearly apparent. The U.S. and British divisions were about equal in the initial stages of OVER-LORD, but once the hold on the Continent was secure, the American preponderance of divisions rapidly became greater. By virtue of the huge stockpiles of American production already established and through his control of the U.S. military manpower buildup on the Continent, General Eisenhower could ensure the acceptance of U.S. staff views on winning the war. The British were forced to recognize the fact and, whatever political orientation the Prime Minister hoped to give the Western Allied military effort, he had to yield.

As the war in Europe drew to a close, the Allies were confronted with the crucial problem of how to defeat Japan. When the Allied forces closed in around Japan in the last year of the conflict, questions of political versus military objectives loomed up. In determining the final strategy against Japan, it became more difficult to separate war from postwar concerns and the desires of partners in the coalition from purely American wishes. Those factors cropped up during the debates over the need for a Pacific OVERLORD. During the fall of

1944 the joint planners in Washington examined various courses of action against Japan and prepared plans for the encirclement and invasion of the home islands. As it turned out later, much of the planning was materially altered or overtaken by events.

The Washington planners believed that after the Okinawa operation, which was scheduled for March 1945, the choice would be between operations against other Ryukyu Islands, Hokkaido, and along the China coast. It was the feeling of the planners that Hokkaido would require too many forces and that weather conditions around the island were very poor. Plans were also prepared for the China coast area despite the difficult terrain and lack of adequate sites for air bases. The planners were especially interested in the future developments of airfields in the Ryukyus, since pressure against Japan could be intensified by air strikes.

During early 1945 detailed plans were prepared by the joint planners for Operation OLYMPIC, the assault on Kyushu, scheduled for Nov. 1, 1945, and for the final assault on Honshu on March 1, 1946. The JCS issued a directive to General MacArthur in May 1945 charging him with the conduct of the campaign against Kyushu and a directive to Admiral Nimitz making him responsible for the naval and amphibious phases of the operation. However, no directive was ever issued for the invasion of Honshu.

During the first six months of 1945, the question of the need to invade Japan was the subject of considerable debate and discussion. The advocates of blockade, bombardment, and encirclement were steadfast in their contention that invasion would not be necessary. In June, President Truman, who had succeeded President Roosevelt in April, requested that a study on the cost in money and casualties be prepared to help clarify the situation. Since so many unknown factors and quantities were involved in such an invasion, an accurate estimate could not be prepared, and the President's study was never completed. The Army's recommendation to make plans and preparations for the invasion was accepted as the best way to proceed.

That was the general situation with respect to strategic planning in the coalition war when the atom bombs were dropped on Hiroshima and Nagasaki on the 6th and 9th of August 1945. The dramatic atom-bomb attacks were a complete surprise to the American public—and to the U.S. Army strategic planners, with the exception of the three senior officers in the Operations Division who were in on the well-kept secret. If the disclosures of the postwar atomic spy trials, as reported in *The New York Times* in March 1951, were accurate, the Russians were far better informed on the

U.S. development of the bomb than the Army's strategic planners. Under those circumstances it is understandable why the Army planners were still involved in more or less conventional planning for a war that came to an unconventional and abrupt end. In a way, the termination of strategic planning by a revolutionary development in weaponry was a fitting climax to a war that had defied the Army planners from the beginning and that had shown a tendency to go its own way. Thereafter, the most destructive weapon then known to man would have to be taken into consideration by the strategic planners.

The Pacific OVERLORD assault was never mounted, and no follow-up invasion of the Japanese homeland occurred. In contrast to the European approach to "soften them up by air, then attack by land," the Pacific advance showed the ground forces winning air bases to permit Japan's "Inner Zone" to be bombed. The predominance of the Army and Army Air Forces in Europe was supplanted by the Navy and Army Air Forces in the Pacific, where the Army ground and service forces played extremely important but less dramatic roles. If the atom bomb had failed, however, and an invasion had been necessary, the Army planners would have been negligent had they failed to have plans and preparations under way. It is also worthy of note that irrespective of the kinds of warfare fought during World War II—mass concentration and invasion in Europe, or bombardment, island-hopping, and blockade in the Pacific—both required a vast outlay of U.S. resources and military manpower. The difficulties of fighting a secondary and limited war in the far Pacific at the end of a very long line of communications, and without launching a Pacific OVERLORD and follow-up invasion, had been impressed on the Army planners more and more before the war against Japan ended.

The delicate political problem of Soviet intentions in the Far East was also a consideration in the question of invading Japan. U.S. military leaders generally believed that if an invasion were necessary, it would be desirable to have the Soviet forces pin down the Japanese in northern China, Manchuria, and Korea. General Marshall and the Army staff considered that premise and, in terms of the possible savings in American lives, they were anxious to have the U.S.S.R enter the war against Japan. Details as to the terms and timing of Soviet entry were still unknown during OCTAGON. Shortly after the Quebec conference, General Thomas T. Handy, OPD, informed General Marshall that, in his opinion, continued U.S. military success against Japan and a statement of American postwar intentions on the Asiatic mainland would force the Soviet Union to enter the war in order to secure a seat at the peace table and present its own demands.

In October 1944 at the Moscow Conference, the United States had agreed to establish stockpiles in the Far East in preparation for Soviet entry. Premier Stalin and President Roosevelt agreed upon the terms for Soviet entry. Premier Stalin again told Ambassador Harriman that the Soviet Union would enter the war against Japan two or three months after Germany was defeated and Soviet forces in the Far East were reinforced. At Yalta Premier Stalin and President Roosevelt agreed upon the terms for Soviet intervention: The U.S.S.R. would get Sakhalin and the Kuril Islands; Port Arthur would be leased to the U.S.S.R. and Dairen would become a free port; the Soviet lease on the Manchurian railroads would be revived, and Outer Mongolia would remain autonomous. The Soviet Union announced its readiness to conclude a "pact of friendship and alliance" with the "National Government of China" in order to support China in the war against Japan.

President Roosevelt assumed the responsibility for informing Chiang Kai-shek of the terms and for securing Chiang's approval. Admiral Leahy later commented that there appeared to be little discussion between the President and the Premier on the matter. Had the Russians participated in the Pacific war for a longer period, perhaps the later outburst of indignation against those concessions might not have been so great. But since there was no invasion, and the Japanese surrender on Aug. 14 occurred so quickly after Soviet entry into the war (Aug. 8), the belief that the Russians had duped the Americans gained widespread acceptance in the Western countries as the rift with the U.S.S.R. expanded in the postwar years.

Differences among the coalition partners, which were later considered to have originated at the Yalta Conference, were beginning to appear during 1944. The first differences arose between the two Western Allies. The apparent intentions of the British to foster the conservative elements in liberated nations such as Belgium, Italy, and Greece were not received enthusiastically in the United States, which considered the Atlantic Charter as the guide to be used in determining such future governments. The British role in the war against Japan and the restoration of former colonial territories in the Far East were other areas of disagreement in 1944. Still another point of dissent was the need for continuing Lend-Lease to support the British economy, particularly after the end of the European war. But both the British and the Americans were concerned over Soviet designs toward Poland, Iran, and the Balkans and their intentions in the Far East. As the common bond of danger weakened, and the need for cooperation among the Big Three diminished, further evidence of wrangling and controversy appeared. Just before OCTAGON, General Eisenhower warned General Marshall, "As signs of victory appear in the air, I note little instances that seem to indicate that Allies cannot hang together so effectively in prosperity as they can in adversity."

Slowly the divergent national objectives and war aims of the Allies began to be revealed—objectives theretofore obscured by the common danger the partners had shared, the unconditional surrender slogan, and the political declarations to which they had subscribed. The unconditional surrender concept, which President Roosevelt had announced at the Casablanca Conference in January 1943, had been consistently advanced at the midwar conferences through OCTAGON as the agreed aim of the Allies in the war. The fading of the common danger subjected the unconditional surrender formula, whatever its merits as a rallying point for the Allies in midwar, to the harsh realities of conflicting postwar national political objectives. Born in wartime and directed to the surrender of the enemies, the doctrine offered no common peace aim or basis for the peace settlement.

As time went on the coalition war became increasingly political, and the disagreements and differences that had appeared earlier began to take shape as the Allied victory neared. The shift in the balance of power between the United States and Great Britain and between the U.S.S.R. and the Western Allies, which was evident at OCTAGON, was the forerunner of the day when the West would polarize around the United States and the East around the U.S.S.R. In the last year of World War II the representatives of the United States and the U.S.S.R. would meet eye to eye as the advance guard of the two nations emerging from the conflict as the most powerful in the world, yet whose relations—which were so important for future peace or war—lacked direction and purpose.

Signs of unrest also began to appear on the home front. As victory drew closer, elements within the civilian population, which had remained silent during the early days when the Allied war effort was having a difficult time, would again make themselves heard. Now that the danger was passing, the isolationists would again clamor for the United States to withdraw from foreign entanglements and take care of its own affairs; economy-minded legislators would once more begin to examine the military budget with a critical eye and demand cutbacks and savings in production and appropriations; and parents, wives, and other relatives would become more vocal in expressing their desire to "get the boys back home." The comparatively free and easy days of defeating the enemy would give way to the pressures of approaching peace.

The Army still had to cope with the immense problem of what to do with the defeated enemy countries as well as with the friction being generated on the foreign and domestic fronts. The questions of administrative organization, government, economic aid, and psychological readjustments were only a few of the facets of the impending occupation. During most of 1945, the Army planners were involved with surrender terms and the initiation of the occupation of both Germany and Japan.

The responsibilities thrust upon General Marshall and his staff during the final year of the war became more and more political. The question of how many and which postwar bases the United States would seek to maintain, a subject of considerable concern to the Army and Navy since 1943, came up for determination. Although the President and his military advisers agreed upon the necessity for postwar American control of the Japanese mandated islands, it was the President's wish that U.S. trusteeship be acquired through the United Nations rather than by right of conquest and occupation. The question of bases in the Philippines presented a different problem because the islands were soon to become completely independent of the United States. Negotiations with the Filipino leaders continued through the balance of the war, with the Army and the Navy both vitally interested in the outcome.

The shift from the strictly military to the politico-military phase of the war was a gradual process. It became evident after the Moscow Conference and expanded rapidly during 1944. It has been argued that the SEXTANT Conference not only marked a modification in the political balance of postwar Europe in favor of the U.S.S.R., but also changed the political balance in Asia in favor of the U.S.S.R., or at least against Nationalist China.

The effect that the revelation at SEXTANT of the divergence in thinking between the Western Allies over the importance of China's war role might have had on the Soviet Union's postwar policy for Asia remains to be written. It is apparent that at Tehran Premier Stalin was made aware of the current differences of opinion between the British and the Americans over operations in Burma. It is reported that shortly after President Roosevelt arrived at Tehran the Premier visited with him in his quarters in the Soviet Embassy. At that first meeting between the two wartime heads of government, the only others present were the two interpreters, Charles E. Bohlen and Vladimir N. Pavlov. During their conversation the President is reported to have told Premier Stalin of his conversations with Chiang Kai-chek and the plans for offensive operations in Burma. Churchill stated in his postwar memoirs, "The fact that the President was in private contact with Marshal Stalin and dwelling at the Soviet Embassy, and that he had avoided ever seeing me alone since we left Cairo . . . led me to seek a direct personal interview with Stalin."

At the private audience with the Soviet Premier on Nov. 30, during which he endeavored to make the British position on strategy clear to the Soviet leader, Churchill stated his lack of enthusiasm for "an amphibious operation in the Bay of Bengal" for which the Americans were pressing. He also mentioned how much sooner Japan would be defeated if the U.S.S.R. entered the war in the Pacific. The decisions of the SEXTANT Conference were summarized and sent by the President and the Prime Minister to the Premier at the close of the meetings in Cairo. Despite the general wording of the summary, it was quite clear that the Generalissimo would not get the amphibious operation he had wanted and that the Americans had urged upon Churchill.

It is a matter of speculation whether the American insistence on treating China as a great power at the Moscow Conference, and the failure of the Western Allies at SEXTANT to agree to support that position and follow through with large-scale military operations, were carefully noted by the Kremlin leaders for future reference and possible action.

In any event, the politico-military phase of the war became preeminent after OCTAGON. From that point forward, agreement among the Allies on military plans and war strategy would become less urgent than the need to arrive at acceptable politico-military terms on which the winning powers could continue to collaborate. It would require considerable adjustment of Army staff planning and procedures to handle those new challenges after building up a staff organization trained and experienced in the predominantly military activity of waging a global and coalition war. It had taken the military staff almost three years of war to build and perfect the military machine for the successful assault and invasion of the Continent. All their planning in the midwar period had been directed at accomplishing the decisive blow that had been a primary feature of their strategic concept.

The Western Allies had hardly started their drive across France when the problems of victory and peace were thrust upon the Army planners. They began the last year of the war with the coalition disintegrating, President Roosevelt failing in health, and no successor fully prepared, and with a smoothly functioning, established politico-military machine completely lacking. The widening gaps in U.S. national policy would be added to the growing vacuums in international collaboration, and it appeared that the military staffs would inherit—by default—problems no longer easily divided into military and political categories, and for which little or no provision had been made.

The U.S. strategic planners had been successful in shifting from an era of prewar isolationism to a period of intense coalition experience. But after the summer of 1944 the Army, which had skillfully completed its planning, organization, and preparations for the invasion of the European Continent, was confronted by a new planning environment. Strategic plans and the related factors—the manpower balance and troop basis, budgets, bases, organization of national defense, deployment and production plans, and relations with foreign powers and with a new international organization—would have to be worked out as the Army staff searched for a new basis for national security in the postwar world.

In World War II the alignment of logistics and strategy was a complex, never-ending process. It would be just as erroneous to say that logistical factors were the sole determinants of strategic decisions as to say that the strategic planners were not constantly limited and bound by the realities of the logistical processes. In the first phase of the war, scarcities of both matériel and shipping thwarted Allied planners at every turn. In the last stage almost every article in the catalogue was in plentiful supply for a one-front war, but the timing of the decisive blow was still controlled by the logistical processes involved in moving various portions of the military machine into place. Items in short supply succeeded one another as limiting factors. First it was merchant shipping, then assault shipping; in the final stage it was military manpower and reception and clearance capacity within overseas theaters.

Despite all the debates, discussions, and controversies that occurred throughout the war at national and international meetings, what resulted was a balanced strategy fundamentally in line with the resources available for pursuit, and that the logistical effort was consequently channeled in the right direction and was reasonably economical and efficient despite the waste that must inevitably accompany war. Flexibility in adjusting to circumstances and in making allocations among many theaters and nations in a multifront coalition was one of the principal keys to victory. From another point of view, the dedication of General Marshall and his Army staff to the pursuit of their goal of a decisive military victory to the exclusion of post-war political aims is attested to in the story of the allocation of resources. In the United States, or in its partnership with Great Britain, or in the broad international Lend-Lease area to other members of the United Nations, the allocation of resources was governed by strictly military considerations.

With World War II rapidly approaching an unconventional ending through the new atomic weapon, there were inklings that the roles of the Army, Navy, and Army Air Forces in warfare might be changing, as even the nature of warfare itself might also be changing. No one doubted but that the political and military balance of the world was in a process of continuous flux. As the fighting came to an end, and the civilian wartime Army returned home and was demobilized, the strategic planners began their studies of a new era of unconventional, limited, and general wars.

*   *   *

The conduct of traditional international affairs has become greatly complicated by the twentieth century convergence of several widely differing domestic systems. The contrasting pragmatic, ideological, and charismatic domestic structures of the United States, the U.S.S.R., and the new nations are a major obstacle to a consensus on what is a reasonable solution to an international crisis. Foreign policy decisions are often affected by extremes of bureaucratic empiricism and revolutionary fervor. The danger of international instability in this nuclear age requires that all nations make a greater effort to understand the shortcomings of, and differences in, the various philosophical perspectives of the modern world.

The international system that produced stability in the nineteenth century collapsed under the impact of two world wars; and the age of the superpowers, which temporarily replaced it, is nearing its end. Overwhelming military strength in the nuclear age is no guarantee that a nation can act with decisiveness on the international stage. There appears to be a need to develop a new concept of international order that recognizes that the world has become politically multipolar while remaining militarily bipolar. In the 1940's and 1950's the United States played an important role in providing ad hoc remedies to international instability. In the 1970's perhaps it will have to contribute to a structure that facilitates multipolar initiatives. Coalitions abroad with shared purposes might have to be established. Such regional groupings, supported by the United States, would have to assume a major responsibility for their immediate areas, whereas the United States would be concerned more with the overall framework of order than with the management of every regional undertaking.

If General Marshall were alive today, one wonders how he and his trained, experienced military staff would view such a strategic concept for meeting the challenge of peace.

Appendix I

Glossary of Abbreviations

AAF	Army Air Forces
ABC	American-British Conversations
AFHQ	Allied Force Headquarters
ATC	Air Transport Command
CBI	China-Burma-India Theater
CBO	Combined Bomber Offensive
CCS	Combined Chiefs of Staff
CINCPAC	Commander in Chief, U.S. Pacific Fleet
CINCSWPA	Commander in Chief, Southwest Pacific Area
CMF	Central Mediterranean Forces
COSSAC	Chief of Staff to the Supreme Allied Commander
CPA	Central Pacific Area
CPS	Combined Staff Planners
CSO	Chief Signal Officer
DUKW	2 1/2-ton amphibious truck
ETO	European Theater of Operations
FCNL	French Committee of National Liberation
G-2	Staff Office of Intelligence
G-3	Staff Office of Operations
G-4	Staff Office of Supply
GAF	German Air Force
JCS	Joint Chiefs of Staff
JIC	Joint Intelligence Committee
JLC	Joint Logistics Committee
JPS	Joint Planning Staff or Joint Staff Planners
JSSC	Joint Strategic Survey Committee
JUSSC	Joint U.S. Strategic Committee
JWPC	Joint War Plans Committee

L of C	Line(s) of Communications
Log	Logistics
LST	Landing Ship (Tanks)
MAC	Mediterranean Air Command
MT	Motor Transport
MTO	Mediterranean Theater of Operations
NEI	Netherlands East Indies
OPD	Operations Division
OSS	Office of Strategic Services
PGC	Persian Gulf Command
PGSC	Persian Gulf Service Command
POA	Pacific Ocean Area(s)
RAF	Royal Air Force
RCT	Regimental Combat Team
RN	Royal Navy
SAC	Supreme Allied Commander
SEAC	Southeast Asia Command
SEF	Single-engine fighter aircraft
SHAEF	Supreme Headquarters, Allied Expeditionary Force
SOE	British Special Operations Executive, equivalent to our OSS
SOE/SO	Special Operations Branch of Special Operations Executive
SOPAC	South Pacific Area
SOWESPAC	Southwest Pacific
SWPA	Southwest Pacific Area
U.K.	United Kingdom
USSBS	United States Strategic Bombing Survey
U.S.S.R.	Union of Soviet Socialist Republics
VLR	Very long range
WPD	War Plans Division

Glossary of Code Names

ACCOLADE	Aegean area operations
ANAKIM	Plan for recapture of Burma
ANVIL	Early plan for invasion of southern France
ARCADIA	U.S.–British conference held in Washington, December 1941–January 1942
AVALANCHE	Invasion of Italy at Salerno
BAYTOWN	British invasion of Italy on Calabrian coast
BOLERO	Buildup of U.S. forces and supplies in United Kingdom for cross-Channel attack
BRIMSTONE	Plan for capture of Sardinia
BUCCANEER	Plans for amphibious operation in Andaman Islands
BUTTRESS	British operation against toe of Italy
CHAMPION	Late 1943 plan for general offensive in Burma
CULVERIN	Plan for assault on Sumatra
DIADEM	Full-scale ground offensive launched by the Allied Command in Italy, May 12, 1944
DRAGOON	Final code name for invasion of southern France
EUREKA	International conference at Tehran, November 1943
FRANTIC	AAF shuttle-bombing of Axis-controlled Europe from bases in United Kingdom, Italy, and U.S.S.R.
GOBLET	Invasion of Italy at Cotrone
GYMNAST	Early plan for Allied invasion of Northwest Africa
HUSKY	Allied invasion of Sicily, July 1943

JAEL	Deception plan for OVERLORD
MATTERHORN	Plan for operating B-29s from Cheng-tu against Japan
MILEPOST	Project to build up stocks in the Far East in preparation for the entry of the U.S.S.R. into the war against Japan
MUSKET	Projected landing on heel of Italy near Taranto, 1943
OCTAGON	U.S.–British conference at Quebec, September 1944
OVERLORD	Allied cross-Channel invasion of northwest Europe, June 1944
POINTBLANK	Combined bomber offensive against Germany
PRICELESS	Post-HUSKY Mediterranean operations
QUADRANT	U.S.–British conference at Quebec, August 1943
RANKIN	Plans for return to the Continent in the event of deterioration of the German position
RAVENOUS	4 Corps plan for recapture of northern Burma
RECKLESS	Assault force for Hollandia operation
ROUNDHAMMER	A cross-Channel operation intermediate in size between SLEDGEHAMMER and ROUNDUP
ROUNDUP	Plan for major U.S.–British cross-Channel operation, 1943
SEXTANT	International conference at Cairo, November and December 1943
SLEDGEHAMMER	Plan for limited cross-Channel attack in 1942
TORCH	Allied invasion of Northwest Africa
TRIDENT	U.S.–British conference held at Washington, May 1943
TROOPERS	Military communication center in London

Appendix III

Minutes of Meetings of COSSAC Mission and JPS Algiers

ALLIED FORCE HEADQUARTERS

20 October 1943

Minutes of first meeting held at AFHQ on 19 October Between COSSAC Mission and J.P.S., AFHQ.

THOSE PRESENT:

Brigadier Thompson	Deputy AC of S, G-3, Chairman.
Brigadier General Chambers	
Lt. Col. Wilson	
Lt. Col. Alms	COSSAC
Major G. Hamilton	
W/Comdr. Robinson	
Captain Power	R.N. [Royal Navy]
Commander Evershed	R.N.
Colonel Donahue	G-4
Colonel Sloane	G-2
Colonel MacCloskey	M.A.C. [Mediterranean Air Command]
Colonel Jenkins	G-3 Plans
Colonel Thurburn	Log Plans
Gp. Capt. Cleland	R.A.F.
Lt. Col. Davis	G-3 Plans
Lt. Col. Reynolds	G-3 Plans
Lt. Col. Conway	G-3 Plans
Major Parker	Log Plans
Major Phillimore	G-3 Plans

174

OPENING REMARKS

1. Brigadier Thompson welcomed the visiting Mission.
2. Brigadier Thompson read out the directives issued to General Eisenhower, a result of the QUADRANT conferences.

It was emphasized that, in accordance with these decisions, the plan for operations against Southern FRANCE had to be submitted to the Combined Chiefs of Staff, coordinated with the SAC, by the 1st of November.

AGENDA

3. The Chairman said that he had the following principal points to raise with the COSSAC Mission during their visit. These were:

   a. *Extent to which COSSAC considered AFHQ could make firm plans in the present situation.*

   It was pointed out that it was very difficult for AFHQ to go beyond the terms of the planning memorandum agreed between COSSAC and representatives of AFHQ.

   b. *Overall Mediterranean strategy.*

   It appeared that guidance would be required as to the general strategy in the Mediterranean for the next six months.

   c. *Size of amphibious assault against Southern FRANCE.*

   COSSAC representatives were informed that the maximum amphibious assault which could be mounted by this headquarters against Southern FRANCE next spring would be one division on a two-brigade front.

   d. *British and U.S. participation in operations against Southern FRANCE.*

   The possibilities or otherwise of American or British Divisions moving into FRANCE with French formations required clarification.

   e. *Command.*

   Further information would be required as to the period of operations at which command of AFHQ forces in Southern FRANCE passes to SAC.

   f. *Scope of AFHQ diversion.*

   COSSAC Mission would be asked whether they expected an actual assault in Southern FRANCE or whether they considered the mounting of as large a threat as possible would suffice.

   g. *Timing.*

Detailed examination as to the timing of AFHQ's contribution to OVERLORD would be necessary.

h. RANKIN.

While no directive has as yet been received by the Allied C-in-C on this subject, it was intended that advantage should be taken of the visit of the COSSAC Mission to discuss RANKIN in as great detail as possible.

DISCUSSION.

4. General Chambers said that COSSAC Headquarters wished to see the outline of AFHQ's diversion against Southern FRANCE prior to submission to the Combined Chiefs of Staff. General Chambers also stated that COSSAC expected that the outline plan submitted to the Combined Chiefs of Staff should be reasonably firm, though the actual details would, of course, be left to AFHQ to decide. Continuing, General Chambers informed the meeting that the OVERLORD plan had now been approved by the Combined Chiefs of Staff and as a result was now firm, except for detailed planning by lower formations.

OVERLORD Plan.

General Chambers then outlined the OVERLORD plan for the benefit of the meeting.

As a result of this exposition various points of detail of the OVERLORD plan were discussed.

Size of Assault Against Southern FRANCE.

5. The Chairman informed the meeting that it was unlikely that any guarantee could be given as to the definite size of an assault which AFHQ might launch against Southern FRANCE.

General Chambers stated that COSSAC fully appreciated the position. He emphasized that should the Allies be held on the PISA-RIMINI line in Italy, it was realized that the best contribution which AFHQ could make in containing German divisions was by mounting as large a threat as possible. Should the Allies be in control of Northern ITALY, a land attack, together with an amphibious assault was envisaged. In any event, it would be necessary for the C.M.F. to be prepared to move into Southern FRANCE with as many divisions as possible, should the situation permit.

Brigadier Thompson stated that while this headquarters could mount a threat, no firm commitment could be given as to the size of the force that could assault Southern FRANCE.

6. Captain Power asked the Mission how long they expected AFHQ to maintain their threat against Southern FRANCE.

In reply Colonel Wilson stated that they considered the threat should be maintained until D + 21.

Strategic Policy

7. Brigadier Thompson then described briefly the necessity for an overall strategic policy in the Mediterranean, if the two pre-requisite conditions for OVERLORD were to be produced. These conditions were:

a. Reduction of the G.A.F. capacity to maintain effort, particularly S.E.F. effort, in the assault area.

b. Prevention of the number of German divisions capable of operating against OVERLORD exceeding a stated maximum.

It was pointed out that in order to produce condition *b,* our strategy might require the containing of German divisions in Southern FRANCE, ITALY and the BALKANS.

General Chambers was asked as to whether COSSAC was in a position to discuss with AFHQ the general policy to be pursued in ITALY and the BALKANS. In reply, General Chambers said that he considered any comment on this point was outside his terms of reference.

Timing.

8. Captain Power pointed out the difficulties which would arise in timing the threat against Southern FRANCE, since the mounting of any threat would be likely to induce the Germans to move formations into FRANCE to counter a possible assault, whereas if no threat was mounted it might be possible to persuade the Germans not to reinforce Southern FRANCE in any form.

Basis of AFHQ Plan.

9. In connection with the plan to be submitted to the Combined Chiefs of Staff by the 1st of November, Brigadier Thompson stated that it seemed likely that part of the report would consist of a paper on the basis of the agreed planning memorandum, while part would deal with the policy to be adopted in this theater.

Air Forces.

10. Colonel Jenkins suggested that the question of employment of air forces by AFHQ, in conjunction with operation OVER-LORD, had received insufficient attention in the agreed planning memorandum. The Chairman expressed the hope that the visit

of Wing Commander Robinson (COSSAC Mission) would prove fruitful in enlarging on the part which air forces in this theater might play in producing the necessary air conditions as required for OVERLORD. It was explained that the question of reduction of G.A.F. fighting value was now being tackled in a comprehensive program, POINTBLANK.

Timing of Threat Against Southern FRANCE.

11. General Chambers was asked when COSSAC required the threat to Southern FRANCE to become apparent to the Germans. General Chambers agreed to let AFHQ have an answer on this point in the near future.

   On the above subject, Colonel Alms said that COSSAC considered that it would become apparent to the Germans that an assault was being launched from U.K. against Western FRANCE somewhere between D − 40 and D − 30.

   It was agreed by COSSAC representatives and the J.P.S., AFHQ that the closest coordination would be required as to the timing and mounting of the threat against Southern FRANCE.

12. General Chambers was then asked whether he would agree to operations being undertaken in an area other than against Southern FRANCE, should AFHQ consider that more German divisions could be kept out of FRANCE than by the mounting of a threat against that area. General Chambers agreed to obtain an answer to this question at an early date.

Other Commitments.

13. Attention of the meeting was drawn to the fact that it might still be necessary to undertake operations in the AEGEAN once we were established on the PISA-RIMINI line. Operation ACCOLADE is due for reconsideration at a later date.

SUMMARY.

14. Brigadier Thompson summarized the points which had been agreed at the meeting. These were:
   a. That an overall strategic policy in the Mediterranean theater is required in order to create the best conditions for OVERLORD.
   b. General Chambers agreed that COSSAC Mission did not consider themselves qualified to give authoritative views on general strategy, and that the extent to which planning could be coordinated with COSSAC would be limited to Southern FRANCE.

c. The paper submitted to the Combined Chiefs of Staff would in part be on the basis of the agreed planning memorandum and in part on questions of general strategy.

NEXT MEETING.

15. It was agreed that the meeting should be continued at 1045 hours on the 20th of October.

/sgd/   M. C. D. L. REYNOLDS
Lt. Colonel,
G-3 Plans.

*   *   *

ALLIED FORCE HEADQUARTERS

21 October 1943

Minutes of second meeting held at AFHQ on 20 October between COSSAC Mission and J.P.S., AFHQ.

PRESENT:

Same officers as first meeting except that
a. Colonel Archibald and Colonel Hooper attended this meeting.
b. Major Phillimore was not present.

GENERAL.

1. The minutes of yesterday's meeting were reviewed, amended and approved. (These minutes have since been circulated to all concerned.)
2. On suggestion of Brigadier Thompson it was agreed that the basis for the day's discussion should be the memorandum "Mediterranean Operations 1944" which had been agreed in LONDON between COSSAC and representatives of AFHQ.
3. COSSAC Mission handed round for approval a draft telegram addressed to COSSAC Headquarters asking for information on various points. It was agreed that the draft telegram should be dispatched subject to certain amendments.

A copy of this telegram, as amended, is attached to these minutes.

DISCUSSION OF CERTAIN POINTS.

4. *Paragraph 5 (Size of Force)*
Comdr. Evershed pointed out that the build up, whether or not

the Allies were in possession of a port in Southern FRANCE, would be slow in comparison with the rate of build up which one had come to expect in this theater. COSSAC Mission said that they realized that such was the case.

5. *Paragraph 11 (Deception Plan)*
Brigadier Thompson stated that he wished to raise the question of deception plans in general and asked how far the current deception plan was approved.

General Chambers briefly outlined Plan JAEL and cover plans for OVERLORD.

Brigadier Thompson pointed out that if it was agreed that this theater was to produce a threat against Southern FRANCE, our activities would be particularly closely bound up with the working out of the general cover plan. It would be necessary for a senior representative of the cover plan staff to be at AFHQ.

6. *Paragraph 20 (Timing)*
On being questioned, General Chambers stated that COSSAC did not wish any amphibious landing in Southern FRANCE to occur before D day because, apart from other reasons, such action might result in premature rising of Patriot forces.

The Mission was then asked whether COSSAC Headquarters had any objection to an attack overland from Northern ITALY to Southern FRANCE being carried out prior to D day OVER-LORD. In reply General Chambers said that such action might very well prejudice the chances of OVERLORD and as such was not acceptable to COSSAC.

Captain Power pointed out the difficulty of AFHQ having the same D day as OVERLORD and that for various reasons it appeared more suitable that D day for amphibious operations against Southern FRANCE should be after OVERLORD D day.

It was agreed that if an expedition was required to sail against Southern FRANCE, it was most undesirable that it should sail before it was known with certainty that OVERLORD was sailing from U.K.

COMMAND.

7. COSSAC Mission was asked at what stage they considered the Mediterranean forces operating in or against Southern FRANCE would pass to the command of S.A.C.

In reply General Chambers said that the following points would determine the date on which command of ground forces would pass:

a. Establishment of communications.

b. Situation on the ground.

After some discussion it was agreed that any actual landing operations and the establishment of the initial facilities in Southern FRANCE would all be carried out under the command of AFHQ. COSSAC Mission stated that it was unlikely that S.A.C. would assume operational control until forces in Southern FRANCE had advanced sufficiently far for their operations to require coordination with those forces operating in Northern and Western FRANCE.

Wing Comdr. Robinson (COSSAC Mission) suggested that, as U.K. and Mediterranean based air forces might be operating against a common area at an earlier date than would U.K. and Mediterranean based ground forces, the problem of coordinating their action would probably arise sooner than would the coordination of ground forces. Considerable discussion then ensued on this point and it was agreed that further detailed examination of this question would be required at a later stage when coordinating detailed plans.

FRENCH PARTICIPATION.

8. COSSAC Mission was questioned regarding any political considerations governing participation of French forces in assault against Southern FRANCE. It was believed that they objected to such participation in early stages. General Chambers said that the question of whether French forces were suitably trained to take part in an assault and the standard of their security had caused COSSAC Headquarters to feel that they might not be suitable for employment in such a role, but that information on this point in LONDON was somewhat scanty and that COSSAC Mission would like to have information on this subject from AFHQ.

Replying, Brigadier Thompson said that he thought that French troops would not be the best choice for the assault phase. He also mentioned that as they had not yet been brought into planning there were important security complications.

With regard to command of French forces, Brigadier General Chambers said that it had always been envisaged by COSSAC Headquarters that French troops would operate under an American or British commander. If a case should arise where only French troops were put into Southern FRANCE, General Chambers felt it essential there should be a competent Allied Mission with them. Brigadier Thompson concurred in these views. Further discussion brought to light the fact that COSSAC Headquarters had not communicated any information concerning OVERLORD to the French authorities in LONDON and it was pointed out that the position was the same in this theater.

CIVIL AFFAIRS.

9. Brigadier Thompson raised the question of Civil Affairs planning. He pointed out that there obviously must be one coordinated plan applicable to French territory whether occupied by forces entering from the northwest or from the south. Since LONDON was the center of coordination for OVERLORD and connected plans he presumed that a Civil Affairs planning organization would be set up in LONDON. He pointed out that it was essential that AFHQ should be kept very closely informed of all policy and plans in this respect formulated in LONDON and stated, as his personal opinion, that it would probably be most desirable for AFHQ to be represented on any such committee in LONDON so that closest touch would be maintained. General Chambers suggested that until command of forces entering Southern FRANCE from the Mediterranean passed to the S.A.C., Northwest EUROPE, all dealings with the French, if necessary, might be conducted through AFHQ. However, representatives of the Civil Affairs section COSSAC Headquarters were present in ALGIERS and could best speak on this matter. Brigadier Thompson said he did not agree that this would be a workable method since he felt it essential that the governing body of OVERLORD should deal directly with the higher French authorities who might be concerned in the general plans. This view was agreed.

NEXT MEETING.

10. It was agreed that the next meeting would be held at 1045 hours 21 October.

FUTURE DISCUSSIONS.

11. It was agreed that the form for future discussions should be the following:
    a. Meeting to complete discussion of OVERLORD and general points of the agreed planning memorandum.
    b. Meeting to discuss RANKIN.

c. Meeting to examine the draft plan to be submitted by AFHQ to Combined Chiefs of Staff in connection with their diversion for OVERLORD.

/sgd/   M. C. D. L. REYNOLDS
Lt. Colonel,
G-3 Plans.

*   *   *

DRAFT TELEGRAM

Attached to Minutes of
2nd Meeting—COSSAC
Mission & J.P.S. AFHQ

TO: TROOPERS MO 4, please pass to COSSAC

Personal for Major General Bull from Brigadier General Chambers.

1. Preliminary meeting with Head Planners has brought out the following points on which answers are requested:

   a. AFHQ is making an appreciation on the means for the achievement and maintenance of the best possible conditions for OVERLORD. Should this appreciation show that the enemy can best be contained by action in areas other than, and possibly remote from Southern FRANCE, will COSSAC agree to forgo the threat to the South of FRANCE? Such a course may prejudice the early entry of forces through the South of FRANCE should suitable conditions occur sooner than is envisaged in paragraph 13 of Part III OVERLORD.

   b. AFHQ must know by what day, in relation to D day OVERLORD, the conditions necessary for OVERLORD must have been achieved. That is to say what is the latest day on which a decision to launch OVERLORD on the target date or postpone the operation must be taken.

   c. On what day in relation to D day OVERLORD does COSSAC want the threat by AFHQ on Southern FRANCE to become apparent?

   d. What are COSSAC's views on the meaning of the phrase "the necessary air situation" for OVERLORD? Some definition of this phrase is required by AFHQ as a basis on which to assess how they can make the most effective contribution to this end.

2. The following further point was informally put forward:

   AFHQ point out the danger of approving any cover plan for the whole winter period until we are firm on our operational plans for EUROPE as a whole.

*   *   *

ALLIED FORCE HEADQUARTERS

22 October 1943

Minutes of third meeting held at AFHQ on 21 October between COSSAC Mission and the J.P.S., AFHQ.

PRESENT:
    Same as for the first meeting except:
    Captain Power, R.N.
    Lt. Col. Reynolds, G-3 Plans
    Major Phillimore, G-3 Plans.

FRENCH PARTICIPATION.

1. Brigadier Thompson opened the discussion by outlining the memorandum forwarded to the US, British and Russian governments by the French Committee for National Liberation. He explained that although this memorandum had been made available to AFHQ for information only, it was proposed that the J.P.S. would prepare a paper for the Chief of Staff commenting upon the proposals submitted by the French, so that the agreed views of AFHQ might be available if requested by higher authority prior to any decision or action on the part of the three governments concerned.

   Colonel Alms pointed out that the possible employment of French forces in Northern FRANCE would raise such questions as security, administrative and command difficulties, and the movement of French forces at the expense of BOLERO and Mediterranean shipping. He felt that in any case it was most undesirable to employ French forces in the main OVERLORD lodgement area before D + 30. Should it be decided to employ French forces in Northern FRANCE it was tentatively proposed to introduce them after D + 30 through the ports of NANTES and ST. NAZAIRE from whence they could be used for the capture of PARIS. These formations would then be in a US area, thus simplifying to some extent the maintenance and equipment problems. Col. Alms pointed out that, in this case, French forces would be committed directly from North AFRICA and not stage through the U.K. The most desirable method, however, remained as laid down in the OVERLORD plan, i.e., the use of French forces as a whole in Southern FRANCE.

In reply to a query as to whether North African ports would support the additional shipping commitment of moving French forces to BISCAY ports, Col. Jenkins expressed the opinion that CASABLANCA and at least a part of ORAN should be available by the time contemplated for this move. It was agreed however that the movement problems would require more examination. He added his views that, over and above the political considerations involved, the commitment of two or three French divisions into Western FRANCE might be desirable from a tactical viewpoint; that should additional forces be urgently required to support operations in Western FRANCE it would be quicker to introduce French forces from North AFRICA than it would be to bring formations from the US.

Col. Donahue agreed with Col. Jenkins and stated that direct shipments from the US to ITALY should alleviate to some extent the crowded conditions in North African ports.

Brigadier Thompson summarized this discussion and emphasized that there must be close liaison between AFHQ and COSSAC regarding the possible use of French divisions in Western FRANCE to insure that both headquarters do not earmark the same formations for the two areas concerned and to provide a solution to the movement requirements which will be satisfactory to all concerned.

2. For the information of the COSSAC group, the AFHQ planners described the equipment and training program of the French Naval, Ground and Air forces.

AIRFIELDS IN CORSICA.

3. General Chambers requested information as to the status of airfields in CORSICA. Gp. Capt. Cleland explained that although only one fighter field is now operable, others are scheduled to be prepared as opportunity occurs, some of which will be prepared to take medium bomber types. This is not yet on high priority and is governed by the availability of shipping, priority for which goes to the Italian mainland. Gp. Capt. Cleland added that, although there are as yet no firm plans for the development of air bases in CORSICA, it should be possible to establish all landing strips and essential facilities required, within six weeks from the time the order to do so was given.

General Chambers said that, in view of the possibility of RAN-

KIN conditions arising at any time between now and the target date for operation OVERLORD, he considered the early establishment of airfields on CORSICA to be highly desirable and would like to emphasize this point on behalf of COSSAC.

SOE/SO PARTICIPATION.

4. Speaking of the broad strategic aspects of SOE/SO operations in FRANCE, Brigadier Thompson discussed a memorandum received from SOE headquarters in LONDON concerning the extent to which SOE/SO activities might assist the operations in Southern FRANCE in support of OVERLORD. Brigadier Thompson said that he disagreed with the suggestion that southward movement of German formations should be impeded. It was his opinion that the interference with German troop movements should be carried out in order to prevent or delay their movement *northward* rather than hinder their concentration to meet the Mediterranean threat; in other words, every effort should be made to draw German forces to South FRANCE and then to introduce subversive measures designed to prevent their return to oppose the OVERLORD forces.

Brigadier Thompson also pointed out that the SOE paper outlines possible contributions which might be made in case of:

a. A threat, *or*

b. A landing.

He stated that since the present basis for operational planning was a threat which *might* later turn into an assault, SOE/SO measures should be designed to conform to this concept.

Brigadier Thompson summarized the foregoing remarks by saying that the SOE/SO plan must be predicated upon, and co-ordinated with, the overall plans of COSSAC and AFHQ.

OBJECTIVE OF AMPHIBIOUS ASSAULT.

5. Brigadier Thompson pointed out that the paper concerning Mediterranean participation in OVERLORD, which was prepared in U.K., suggested that the actual point of landing under Case Two (in conjunction with an overland advance from Northern ITALY) would be in the CANNES-NICE area. He said that the AFHQ planners can envisage certain conditions where a landing in the TOULON area would be preferable.

Colonel Wilson explained that the subject paper had been so worded because it was felt that the forces advancing overland from Northern ITALY would probably require close support from the amphibious forces because of the fact that the difficult terrain in that area greatly favored the defense. Should the two elements fail to be in close proximity to each other they might be liable to defeat in detail.

Col. Jenkins acknowledged the merit of these considerations but pointed out that one must also consider the possibility that RANKIN conditions might prevail at the time OVERLORD is mounted. In such circumstances we should strive to make our initial landing in the TOULON area.

Brigadier Thompson explained that for these reasons an examination is in fact being made of all possible beaches in Southern FRANCE so that AFHQ will be prepared to exploit any favorable opportunity to assault directly into the target area.

COSSAC–AFHQ.

6. General Chambers asked AFHQ's views on what liaison arrangements should be established between COSSAC and AFHQ in order to facilitate the further development of plans within each headquarters. Brigadier Thompson replied that this matter would be given further consideration by the J.P.S., after which a reply would be made to General Chambers' question.

SERVICE TROOPS.

7. Brigadier Thompson pointed out that port units and other administrative formations might well prove a serious limiting factor affecting the movement of Mediterranean forces far into Southern FRANCE.

Col. Thorburn agreed and stated that there will not be enough L of C troops to serve an overland advance north-eastwards from ITALY and, at the same time, an amphibious operation into Southern FRANCE.

General Chambers stated that, in view of the QUADRANT decision that where there is a shortage of resources, available resources should be disposed toward insuring the success of OVERLORD, he would like to have on the record that COSSAC considers the introduction of Mediterranean troops into Southern FRANCE, as soon as conditions permit, an essential to the OVERLORD plan.

NEXT MEETING.

8. It was agreed that the next meeting would be held on Friday, 22 October 1943 at 1045 hours to discuss operation RANKIN.

/sgd/   R. WARREN DAVIS
Lt. Colonel, G.S.C.,
G-3 Plans.

*   *   *

ALLIED FORCE HEADQUARTERS

23 October 1943.

Minutes of fourth meeting held at AFHQ on 22 October between COSSAC Mission and J.P.S., AFHQ.

PRESENT:

Brigadier Thompson	Deputy AC of S, G-3, Chairman
Brigadier General Chambers	
Lt. Col. Wilson	
Lt. Col. Alms	COSSAC
Major G. Hamilton	
W/Comdr. Robinson	
Colonel Jenkins	G-3 Plans
Colonel Donahue	G-4 Plans
Gp. Capt. Cleland	M.A.C.
Colonel MacCloskey	M.A.C.
Colonel Sloane	G-2
Commander Evershed	R.N.
Lt. Col. Conway	G-3 Plans
Lt. Col. Davis	G-3 Plans
Lt. Col. Reynolds	G-3 Plans
Major Roney-Dougal	Log Plans

RANKIN CONDITIONS.

1. General Chambers discussed briefly the background of COSSAC planning for RANKIN and pointed out that RANKIN conditions might occur at any time from now onwards.

OUTLINE PLANS FOR RANKIN.

2. Lt. Col. Alms described the various courses of action contemplated by COSSAC under conditions A, B and C, respectively. He described certain defensive measures currently being taken by

the Germans in Northern FRANCE, as a result of which it appears that operations under condition A can not be undertaken until the return of favorable weather, i.e., in April 1944. Preparations for OVERLORD would have reached such an advanced stage by that time that RANKIN Case A would be OVERLORD but possibly with the target date slightly advanced.

Commander Evershed stated the opinion that no landing against opposition can be mounted in the Gulf of Lions during the winter. Weather conditions in the Gulf at this time of year are most unpredictable and will continue to be so until the end of April.

PERIOD OF WARNING FOR RANKIN.

3. Brigadier Thompson pointed out that AFHQ might be faced with the problem of meeting two possibly conflicting requirements for Mediterranean forces, i.e., those attending operations in ITALY and those arising from any AFHQ obligation to support RANKIN at short notice. It was important, therefore, to know what period of warning AFHQ might expect before D day of the respective RANKIN operations. Lt. Col. Wilson replied that the period of warning on which COSSAC is planning for the infusion of the main forces in Case B is 42 days, the basis for this being the time required to assemble the necessary shipping. For Case C RANKIN, Lt. Col. Alms stated that COSSAC is considering a period of 14 days, the Staff Duties requirements being the governing factor. Both periods are dependent upon the greatest possible amount of preplanning having been achieved.

It was agreed that Case A RANKIN so nearly conforms to OVERLORD that planning for Case A will follow in general the same lines as those of the OVERLORD operation. As discussed earlier in the meeting, RANKIN A cannot be mounted until the return of favorable weather conditions in the ENGLISH Channel.

COMPOSITION OF FORCES IN
SOUTHERN FRANCE—RANKIN.

4. Brigadier Thompson asked why COSSAC press so strongly for the initial force committed to Southern FRANCE in Case B RANKIN be one US and one British division, and emphasized that such an arrangement would introduce major difficulties in administration, particularly as the operation would be mounted in a great hurry. He asked if it would not be better to try to take a Corps complete with its HQ.

In this regard, Colonel Jenkins emphasized these difficulties and expressed his view that AFHQ might not, in fact, have fully refitted US or British divisions available at the time required.

General Chambers stated that COSSAC does propose that French forces be accompanied by at least one US and one British division. He added that, should further examination of the problem by AFHQ indicate that this will not be feasible, one or the other should be included and that, in any case, US or British command will be essential.

AIRBORNE FORCES—RANKIN.

5. Brigadier Thompson asked whether COSSAC contemplates that all airborne operations will be directed from U.K., in view of the present policy of concentrating almost all airborne forces there.

Wing Comdr. Robinson expressed the view that, because of the distances involved in some cases, as, for example, a possible airborne landing to seize Vichy, it would not be feasible to control all airborne forces from U.K.

Lt. Col. Alms stated that plans will be made for the use of airborne forces based in U.K. to seize certain important points in the north. The execution of more distant tasks, e.g., the seizure of VICHY, has not yet been considered in detail.

Brigadier Thompson mentioned that AFHQ would, under Case C RANKIN (complete surrender), have very considerable tasks in its own theater, quite apart from any assistance in FRANCE. The disarming of, say, 25 German divisions in Northern ITALY was an example. AFHQ might desire to transport forces by air to strategic points at which enemy formations returning to GERMANY from Northern ITALY might be intercepted and disarmed. This might be the primary call on our airborne resources.

AFHQ COMMITMENTS FOR RANKIN.

6. Brigadier Thompson mentioned that, as AFHQ had not received its directive concerning its part in RANKIN operations, the discussion conducted during this meeting was primarily of an exploratory nature; firm commitments in this regard could not, therefore, be given at this time.

There followed a discussion concerning the practicability of delineating the various RANKIN conditions. It was generally agreed that these conditions would be fluid, but that, for planning purposes, the definitions enunciated by COSSAC were appropriate.

Brigadier Thompson then obtained confirmation from the

COSSAC representatives that they hoped that AFHQ would make the following contribution to RANKIN:

a. Case A—As for OVERLORD.

b. Case B—Mediterranean forces to land in an undefended, but demolished port in Southern FRANCE as soon as possible after German withdrawal therefrom has occurred.

c. Case C—Depends upon higher decision as to AFHQ's role elsewhere than in Southern FRANCE under RANKIN C conditions, but in any case all available French forces and if feasible US and British forces as specified in para. 4 above should be introduced into Southern FRANCE.

SIGNIFICANCE OF VICHY.

7. Colonel Jenkins said that in his opinion too much emphasis appears to be placed on the importance of seizing VICHY rather than pursuing enemy forces. It was his view that political considerations could and should attend the completion of the military requirements and that the forces sent into Southern FRANCE should not, therefore, be hindered by an inflexible directive to secure the VICHY area.

Lt. Col. Alms said that COSSAC was as yet without guidance on the importance of VICHY but the likelihood of its seizure warranted some preparation; he would, on his return to U.K., have Colonel Jenkins' suggestion examined further by the COSSAC planners.

COMMAND.

8. General Chambers called attention to the fact that, under RANKIN C, the SAC would probably delegate command authority for the US sphere of control to the senior US commander in the field. Such action would create the need for a different communication set-up. General Chambers said that Brigadier General Lanahan, Deputy CSO for COSSAC, would arrive at AFHQ to discuss this and allied matters.

NEXT MEETING.

9. An AFHQ J.P.S. meeting was tentatively scheduled for 1630 hours 23 October in order to discuss a draft of the report required by the CCS.

/sgd/   R. WARREN DAVIS
Lt. Colonel, G.S.C.
G-3 Plans.